ACROSS CANADA

Resources and Regions

SECOND EDITION □ STUDENT WORKBOOK

Christine Hannell
B.Sc., M.Sc., B.Ed.
Brampton Centennial Secondary School

Robert Harshman
B.A., M.A., B.Ed.
Applewood Heights Secondary School

John Wiley & Sons
Toronto   New York   Chichester   Brisbane   Singapore

Canadian Cataloguing in Publication Data
Hannell, Christine
Across Canada, 2nd edition. Student workbook

Supplement to: Hannell, Christine. Across Canada.
2nd ed.
ISBN 0-471-79667-0

1. Canada - Description and travel - 1981 -
I. Harshman, Robert. II. Title.

FC75.H322 1987   917.1
C87-093518-6
F1017.H322 1987

Typesetting by Jay Tee Graphics Ltd.
Printed and bound in Canada
10 9 8 7 6 5 4 3 2 1

CONTENTS

To the Student

1 An Overview of Canada and How It Relates to the World   1

2 Canada's Physical Base   24

3 Our Human Heritage   94

4 Where We Live   113

5 Farming in Canada   136

6 Water   158

7 Energy and Transportation   180

8 Our Natural Resources and How We Use Them   201

9 Canada's Industries   234

10 Canada and Its Regions   254

TO THE STUDENT

This workbook has been written especially for you. We hope that you will find it interesting to use and that it will be very valuable when it comes to test and examination time.

You will find that the exercises, information maps, and diagrams are in the same order as in the textbook. Sometimes the questions are the same as in the text, but often they are different.

At the front of each chapter there are boxes where you can put a check mark when your teacher assigns a section of work. When you have completed that section, you can check the second box so you will know how far you have progressed.

In the margin, the numbers in italics refer to the page number in the text. You will be able to find the relevant pages for finding the answers quickly.

Games and crossword puzzles should help you to enjoy getting your Geography credit.

HAVE FUN!

AN OVERVIEW OF CANADA AND HOW IT RELATES TO THE WORLD

1

PERSONAL PROGRESS CHART

Put a check mark in the first square for each section when your teacher assigns it. When you have completed the section, put a check mark in the second square.

Page	Topic	Assigned by teacher	Completed by you
2	Canada's Physical Regions	☐	☐
4	Canada's Provinces	☐	☐
5	Labelling a Map of Canada	☐	☐
6	Canada and the World	☐	☐
6	Population Density	☐	☐
9	Canada's Trade with Other Countries	☐	☐
10	Value of Canada's Imports and Exports	☐	☐
11	Tariffs	☐	☐
13	Transportation of Our Imports and Exports	☐	☐
14	Latitude and Longitude	☐	☐
18	Time Zones in Canada	☐	☐
20	Other Ways in Which Canada Reacts with the World	☐	☐
22	Vocabulary Crossword	☐	☐

CANADA'S PHYSICAL REGIONS

p. 2

1. Fill in the blanks.

I live in _____, which is located in the _____

of _____ which is in the _____ of Cana
    (province or territory)   (which part)

2. Using Figure 1-1 in the textbook, fill in this diagram.

A _____ Across Canada Showing the _____

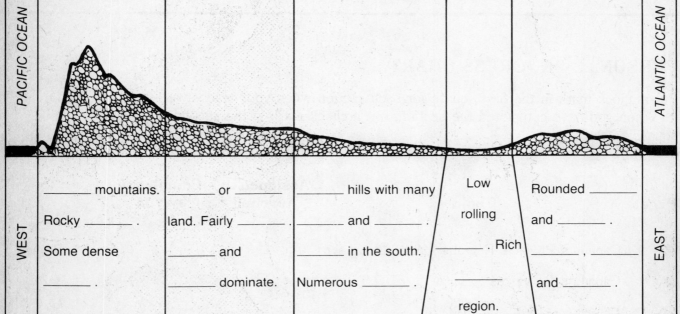

PACIFIC OCEAN

WEST

_____ mountains.

Rocky _____.

Some dense

_____.

_____ or _____

land. Fairly _____.

_____ and

_____ dominate.

_____ hills with many

_____ and _____.

_____ in the south.

Numerous _____.

Low rolling

_____. Rich

_____ region.

Rounded _____

and _____.

_____, _____

and _____.

ATLANTIC OCEAN

EAST

p. 3

3. Using Figure 1-3 in the textbook, colour and name the six physical regions of Canada. _____

4. Examine the two figures you have just finished and then complete the following. Draw a line from each region in the left column to the correct descriptions in the right column.

Western Mountains ●

Interior Plains ●

Canadian Shield ●

Great Lakes–St. Lawrence ● Lowlands

Appalachian Mountains ●

Arctic ●

Quite flat or gently rolling
Most southerly region
Smallest region
Highest point in Canada
U-shaped region
Coldest region
Shortest ocean coastline
No trees
Grassland
Very little vegetation
Touches two oceans
Most easterly region
Rounded hills and mountains

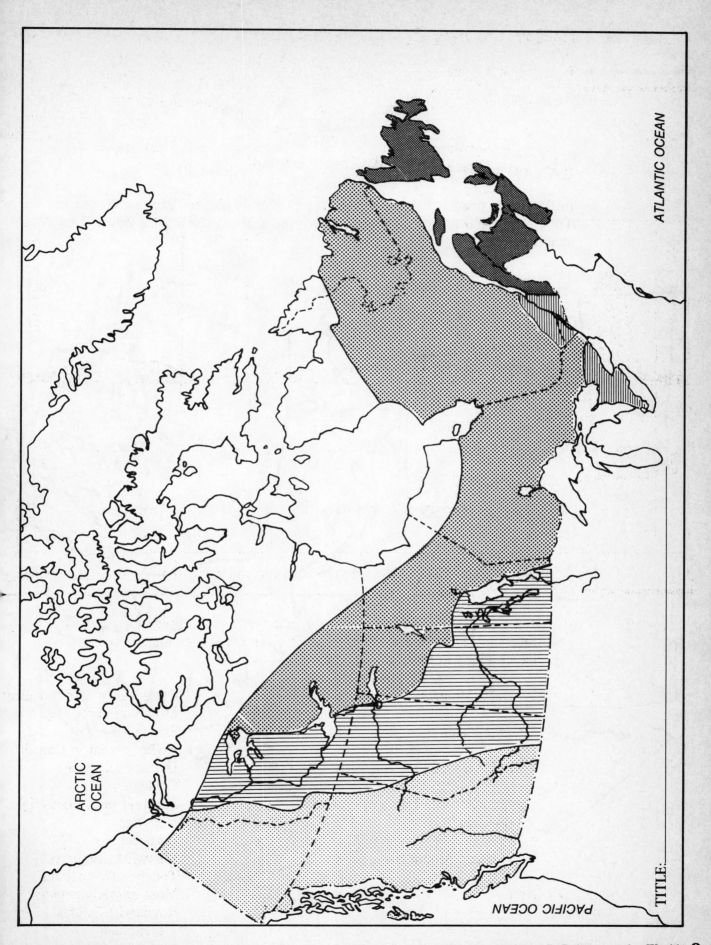

ATLANTIC OCEAN

ARCTIC OCEAN

PACIFIC OCEAN

TITLE:

5. What is a region _____

_____

_____

CANADA'S PROVINCES

In the space provided, label each of the provinces and territories outlined below. They have been turned so that they may be sideways or upside down. Use your atlas for help.

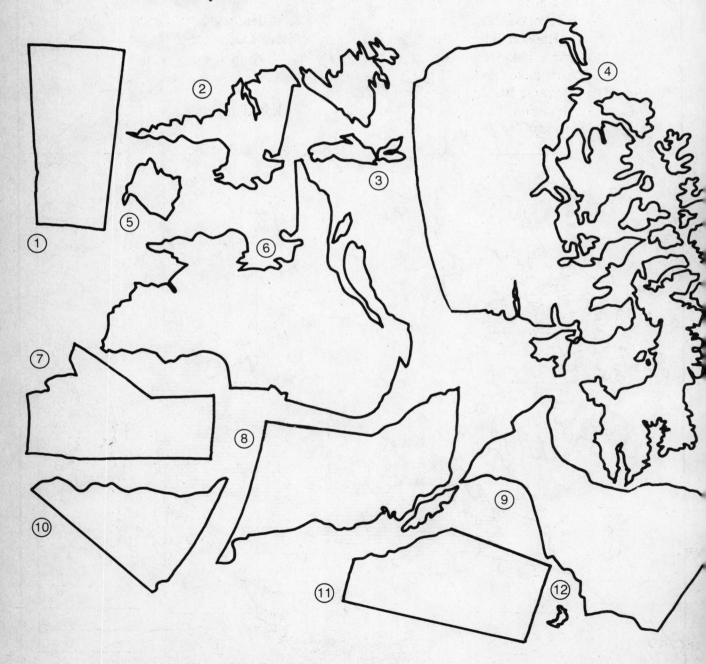

LABELLING A MAP OF CANADA

1. On the map of Canada below, label the following features. Use your atlas as a guide.

   (a) The provinces and territories (Use short forms.)
   (b) Ottawa and the capitals of the provinces and territories (St. John's, Toronto, Edmonton, Yellowknife, Whitehorse, Charlottetown, Fredericton, Halifax, Quebec, Winnipeg, Regina, Victoria)
   (c) These other large cities: Vancouver, Calgary, Windsor, London, Saint John, Kitchener, St. Catharines, Oshawa, Hamilton, Montreal, and Niagara Falls
   (d) These important bodies of water: Pacific Ocean, Atlantic Ocean, Arctic Ocean, Hudson Bay, Great Bear Lake, Great Slave Lake, Lake Athabasca, Lake Winnipeg, Lake Superior, Lake Huron, Lake Michigan, Lake Erie, and Lake Ontario
   (e) These rivers: St. Lawrence and Mackenzie
   (f) Other features: continental U.S.A., Alaska, and Kalaallithvunaat (Greenland)

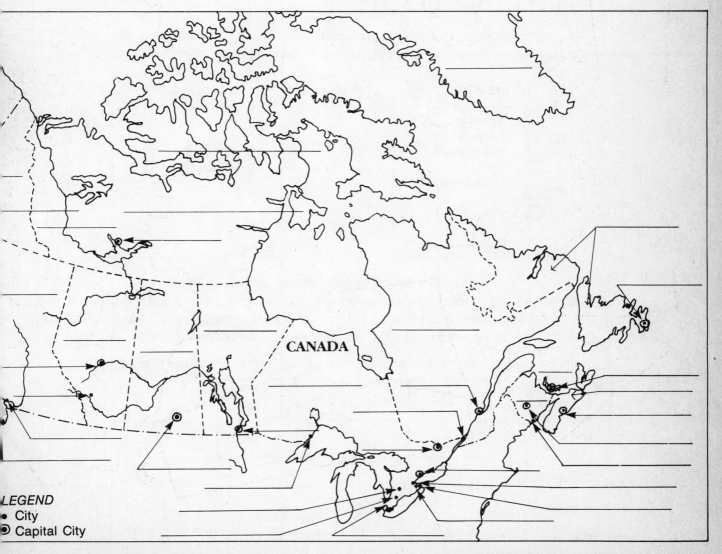

CANADA

LEGEND
• City
☉ Capital City

CANADA AND THE WORLD

p. 5
Figure 1-5 contains information about the five largest countries in the world (as well as other countries).

1. List these countries in order, largest first.

   (a) _____ (d) _____

   (b) _____ (e) _____

   (c) _____

2. Write one or two sentences to describe how Canada's size compares with that of the U.S.S.R. and the U.S.A. _____

   _____

   _____

POPULATION DENSITY

pp. 6-7
Population density varies greatly from one country to another in the world. The chart below illustrates the population density of some countries.

COUNTRY	POPULATION DENSITY (PEOPLE PER SQUARE KILOMETRE)
Australia	2
Canada	2
Bangladesh	685
Brazil	12
United Kingdom	231
Egypt	
Hong Kong	
Italy	
Taiwan	

1. Complete the list by using information in your atlas.
2. Assume that each box below and on the next page represents one square kilometre. Use a capital P to represent one person per square kilometre. Fill in each box with the number of P's for each country on the list.

Start with the country with the lowest population density and end with the highest.

LOWEST
Population
Density

Country _____ _____ _____

Population

Density _____ _____ _____

```
┌─────────┐          ┌─────────┐          ┌─────────┐
│         │ ───────▷ │         │ ───────▷ │         │
│         │          │         │          │         │
└─────────┘          └─────────┘          └─────────┘
```

Country   _____   _____   _____

Population

Density   _____   _____   _____

```
┌─────────┐          ┌─────────┐          ┌─────────┐   HIGHEST
│         │ ───────▷ │         │ ───────▷ │         │
│         │          │         │          │         │   Population
└─────────┘          └─────────┘          └─────────┘   Density
```

Country   _____   _____   _____

Population

Density   _____   _____   _____

Example:

P   P   P   P

Population density is four people per square kilometre.

3.   How does Canada compare in population density with the other countries

     listed? _____

     _____

4.   The area of Canada with the lowest population density that I know of or

     have visited is _____ .

     I have also visited or heard of an area with a much higher population

     density, namely, _____ .

5.   After reading page 6 in the text, explain the meaning of

     (a) sparse _____

          dense _____

     (b) Does sparse or dense best describe Canada's population density? _____

     (c) Is this equally true in all parts of Canada? _____ Explain your

          answer carefully. _____

6. Use this graph to answer question 11 on page 8. Give your graph a title.

Title: _____

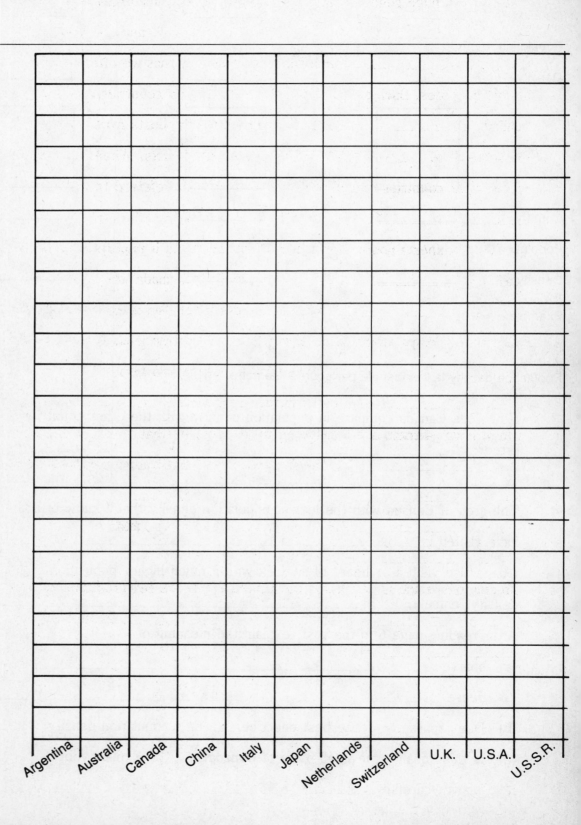

Number
of
People
(millions)

Argentina Australia Canada China Italy Japan Netherlands Switzerland U.K. U.S.A. U.S.S.R.

CANADA'S TRADE WITH OTHER COUNTRIES

pp. 8-13

1. Read pages 8 to 13 in the textbook, and then fill in the blanks in these sentences.

Canada is a huge country with many resources. Raw materials such as

_____ , _____ , and

_____ are important resources that we often sell to

other countries. Such products that we sell to other countries are

called _____ . When we buy products from other

countries, we _____ these products. Whenever we buy

from other countries or sell products to them, it is referred to as

_____ .

If Canada exports goods worth more than the goods it imports, this is

called a _____ . By contrast, Canada has

a _____ when it imports more than it exports. Canada,

of course, always attempts to export more and import less. A trade tariff is

a _____ . The tariff is designed to help

_____ but it hurts _____ .

Our trading partners are considered to be countries that_____

_____ . The five most important trading partners we have

are _____ , _____ ,

_____ , _____ , and

_____ .

To countries such as Japan and the United States we sell products such as

_____ and _____ . In turn we buy

_____ .

1/Canada and How It Relates to the World **9**

2. Fill in the trade balance as well as the last column for this chart. The trade figures are in millions of dollars.

YEAR	EXPORTS	IMPORTS	TRADE BALANCE	DEFICIT OR SURPLUS?
1977	44 554	42 332	2 222	Surplus
1978	52 842	49 938		
1979	64 317	62 871		
1980	74 259	69 128		
1981	80 895	78 665		
1982	90 964	75 485		
1983	84 403	67 630		
1984	112 100	91 700		

VALUE OF CANADA'S IMPORTS AND EXPORTS

1. Using the statistics in the previous chart, complete the following line graph by drawing in the line for imports.

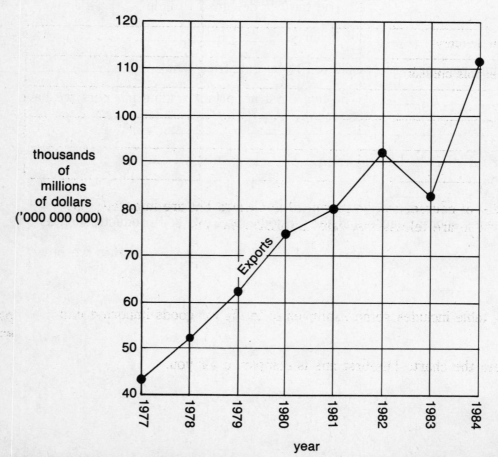

In the completed graph you can see that imports are trailing exports in each of the years. This graph shows you the same information as the previous chart.

2. (a) Which do you find easier to understand: the line graph or the chart? _____

   (b) Explain why (briefly). _____

   _____

3. There are certain products that Canada must import because of its climate, geography, and so on. Also, other countries can sell us products for less than it would cost us to produce them ourselves. From your own experience, which of these products do you think would probably be imports to Canada? Place a check mark in the appropriate column.

PRODUCTS	PROBABLY IMPORTED TO CANADA	PROBABLY NOT IMPORTED TO CANADA
Frozen orange juice		
Newsprint		
Photographic film		
Wheat for bread		
Telephones		
Tomatoes (in January)		
Canned pineapple chunks		
Coconuts		
Textbooks		
Stereos		

Many products, of course, can be produced in Canada but are imported, too. Examples of these are televisions, cars, furniture, and oil.

TARIFFS

The following table includes some examples of tariffs for goods imported into Canada.

pp. 10-11

1. Complete the chart. The first line is completed for you.

ITEM IMPORTED	TARIFF RATE	COST OF ITEM	ACTUAL TARIFF	TOTAL PRICE INCLUDING TARIFF
(a) Television from Japan	12.8%	$ 500	$ 64	$ 564
(b) Small car from France	12.8%	10 000	_____	_____
(c) Wooden chair from the U.S.A.	18.1%	100	_____	_____
(d) Watch from Taiwan	16.7%	50	_____	_____
(e) Toy truck from Hong Kong	17.2%	10	_____	_____
(f) Pair of socks from South Korea	20% + 50¢ per twelve pairs	24 per twelve pairs	_____ per twelve pairs	_____ per twelve pairs
		_____ per pair	_____ per pair	_____ per pair

2. Many people would be affected by a trade tariff on radios imported into Canada. Write one sentence to describe how the following people would feel about such a tariff.

(a) Canadians assembling radios in Mississauga _____

_____

(b) A Japanese radio factory worker _____

_____

(c) A Canadian interested in buying a radio _____

_____

(d) A dock worker in Vancouver who unloads Japanese radios _____

_____

3. Answer question 22 on page 11 of your textbook.

(a) The advantages of free trade between Canada and the U.S.A. would

be _____

_____.

(b) The disadvantages of free trade between Canada and the U.S.A. would

be _____

_____

TRANSPORTATION OF OUR IMPORTS AND EXPORTS

1. Read pages 13 to 16 in your textbook, and then fill in this chart. You will be comparing different methods of transporting cargo.

pp. 13-16

	WHERE IT CAN TRAVEL	WHERE IT CANNOT TRAVEL	EFFECTS OF WEATHER, SEASONS	OTHER ADVANTAGES OR DISADVANTAGES
Truck				
Train				
Ship				
Airplane				

2. **(a)** Transhipment of goods involves the _____ _____ .

p. 15

Much transhipment involves containerized freight, which is _____ _____ .

Containerized freight saves money because _____ _____ .

It also cuts down on crime because _____ _____ .

(b) What special precautions would you have to take if you were packing items in these huge containers? _____ _____ _____

3. List five items that would travel well in such containers and explain why this would be so.

(a) _____

(b) _____

(c) _____

(d) _____

(e) _____

4. List three items that would not travel safely in containers such as these, when travelling for long periods of time.

(a) _____

(b) _____

(c) _____

LATITUDE AND LONGITUDE

pp. 17-20

Latitude and longitude are like a net of lines put over the world. The lines of latitude circle the world as shown in the diagram to the right.

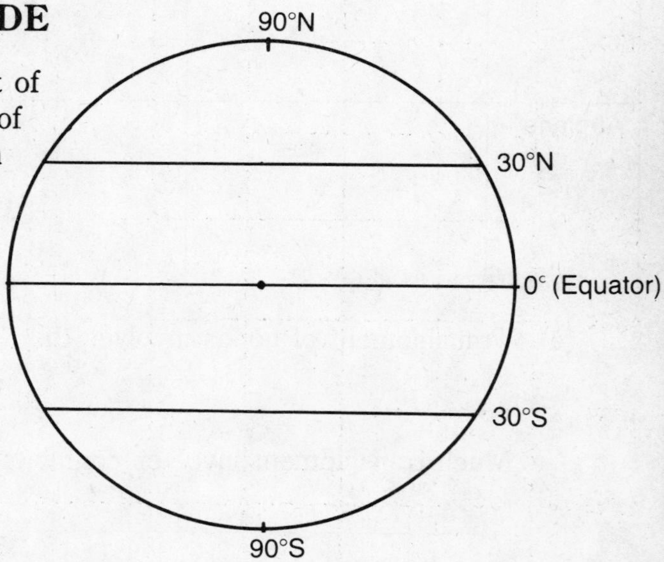

p. 18

1. Add the following lines of latitude: 60°N, 15°S, 60°S, 80°N, 15°N, 80°S. (Use a ruler.)
2. Some important lines of latitude include those listed below:

LINE OF LATITUDE	NAME OF LINE
66.5°N	_____
23.5°N	_____
23.5°S	_____
66.5°S	_____

Lines of longitude cross over at the North and South Poles.

3. They are furthest apart where they cross the _____ .

The 0° line of longitude is called the _____ Meridian.

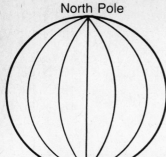

North Pole

South Pole

4. Join each of these points of latitude and longitude *in the order given* to form letters. Join only the points given. The first letter is done for you.

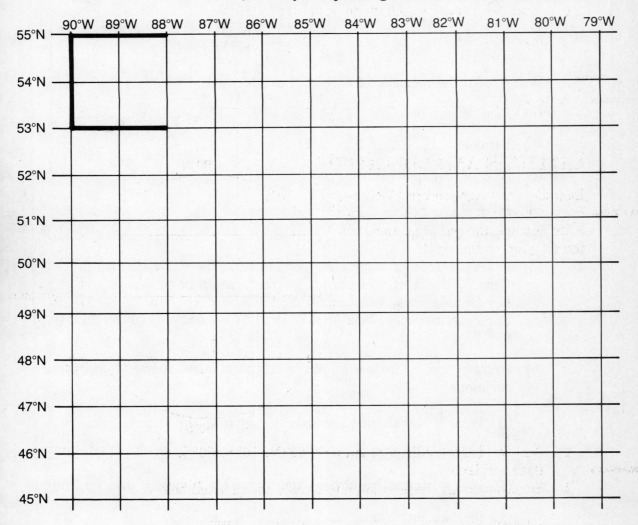

1st letter: 55°N 88°W
55°N 90°W
53°N 90°W
53°N 88°W

2nd letter: 53°N 86°W
55°N 86°W
53°N 84°W
55°N 84°W

3rd letter: 55°N 82°W
55°N 80°W
53°N 82°W
53°N 80°W

4th letter: 52°N 88°W
52°N 90°W
50°N 90°W
50°N 88°W
51°N 88°W
51°N 89°W

6th letter: 50°N 82°W
52°N 82°W
51°N 81°W
52°N 80°W
50°N 80°W

9th letter: 48°N 84°W
46°N 84°W
46°N 83°W
48°N 83°W

5th letter: 52°N 85°W
50°N 85°W
50°N 83°W

7th letter: 48°N 88°W
46°N 88°W

8th letter: 48°N 85°W
48°N 87°W
47°N 87°W
47°N 85°W
46°N 85°W
46°N 87°W

10th letter: 48°N 82°W
46°N 81°W
48°N 80°W

pp. 17-18

5. Write down the meaning of each of these terms.

(a) Line of latitude _____

(b) Latitude _____

(c) Line of longitude _____

(d) Longitude _____

(e) Prime Meridian _____

6. **(a)** Label the lines of latitude and longitude on the following map of Canada. Use a map of Canada in your atlas to help.
For latitude lines, look for: 50°N, 75°N, 45°N, 60°N.
For longitude lines, look for: 80°W, 120°W, 55°W, 140°W, 110°W, 95°W.

(b) Using your map from 6 (a) above and your atlas, answer these three questions:

(i) What is the latitude line used to separate the U.S.A. from western Canada? _____

(ii) Which latitude line divides the four westernmost provinces from the two territories? _____

(iii) Which longitude line separates Saskatchewan and Alberta?

_____

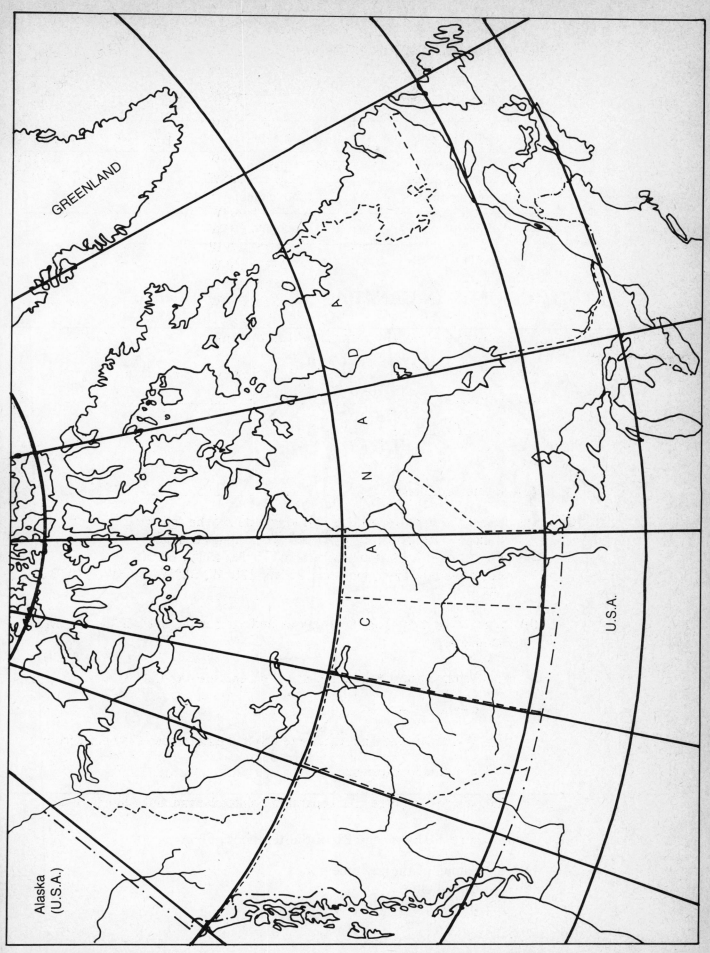

GREENLAND

C
A
N
A
D
A

U.S.A.

Alaska
(U.S.A.)

(c) Using your atlas, fill in this table.

POINT IN CANADA	LATITUDE or LONGITUDE	DESCRIPTION OF ITS LOCATION
Northernmost	(latitude)	
Southernmost	(latitude)	
Westernmost	(longitude)	
Easternmost	(longitude)	

TIME ZONES IN CANADA

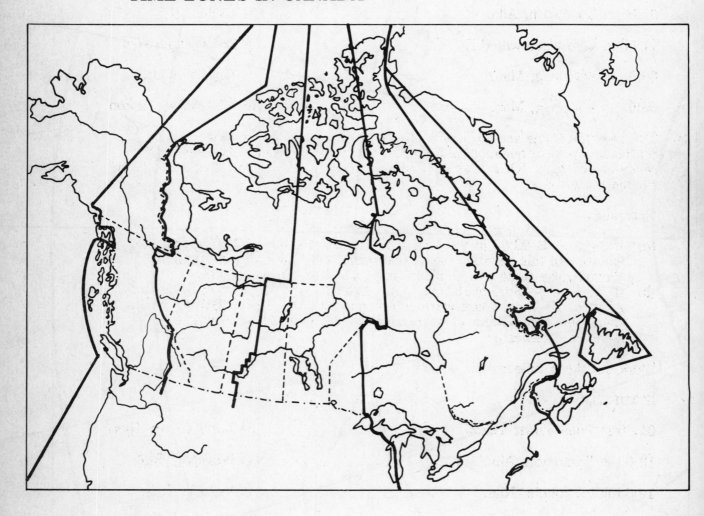

pp. 20-21

1. Using Figure 1-31 on page 21 of the textbook, fill in

   (a) the names of the six time zones

   (b) the capital cities

   (c) the times in each zone as shown

2. Using the map of Canada's time zones on page 21 of the textbook as a guide, fill in the times below.

IF THE TIME IS . . .   THEN THE TIME IS . . .

07:00 in Victoria, B.C.   _____ in Quebec City, Que.

08:00 in Yellowknife, N.W.T.   _____ in St. John's, Nfld.

11:00 in Fredericton, N.B.   _____ in Whitehorse, Yukon

11:30 in St. John's, Nfld.   _____ in Toronto, Ont.

09:00 in Regina, Sask.   _____ in Ottawa, Ont.

07:00 in Victoria, B.C.   _____ in St. John's, Nfld.

08:00 in Edmonton, Alta.   _____ in Halifax, N.S.

11:00 in Charlottetown, P.E.I.   _____ in Fredericton, N.B.

09:00 in Winnipeg, Man.   _____ in Toronto, Ont.

09:00 in Winnipeg, Man.   _____ in Whitehorse, Yukon

3. The next questions are also based on the map on page 21 in your textbook. In these questions, however, the times have been changed from those on the map. (Of course, the differences in time between time zones remain the same.)

Examples:

(a) If the time is 09:00 in Victoria, B.C., then the time is 12:00 in Toronto, Ontario. In this situation, since two hours were added to the time in Victoria, the same two hours must be added to Toronto's time.

(b) If the time is 05:00 in Halifax, N.S., then the time is 02:00 in Edmonton, Alberta. Since six hours were subtracted from the time in Halifax, N.S., then the same number of hours must be subtracted from the time in Edmonton, Alberta.

Work out these times:

IF THE TIME IS . . .   THEN THE TIME IS . . .

01:00 in Whitehorse, Yukon   _____ in Quebec City, Que.

12:00 in Edmonton, Alta.   _____ in Winnipeg, Man.

19:30 in St. John's, Nfld.   _____ in Victoria, B.C.

12:00 in Hamilton, Ont.   _____ in Winnipeg, Man.

13:30 in St. John's, Nfld.   _____ in Calgary, Alta.

17:00 in Fredericton, N.B.   _____ in Quebec City, Que.

18:00 in Regina, Sask.   _____ in Halifax, N.S.

19:00 in Toronto, Ont. _____ in Whitehorse, Yukon

04:00 in Winnipeg, Man. _____ in Vancouver, B.C.

09:00 in Charlottetown, P.E.I. _____ in Yellowknife, N.W.T.

OTHER WAYS IN WHICH CANADA INTERACTS WITH THE WORLD

pp. 22-26

Political Organizations

Fill in the blanks of this chart.

ORGANIZATIONS TO WHICH CANADA BELONGS

ORGANIZATION	SHORT FORM	MAIN AIMS
Commonwealth of Nations		
United Nations		
North Atlantic Treaty Organization		
North American Defence Pact		

Canada's Foreign Aid

p. 25

1. Canada is one of the richest countries in the world. One way to measure this is by the G.N.P. per person, which means _____

   _____

   _____ .

2. Using the graph below, plot bars for the G.N.P. per person in each of these countries: Canada, the United States, Spain, Brazil, Thailand, India, and Burundi. (An example of a bar graph can be found on page 8 of your textbook.)

Title: _____

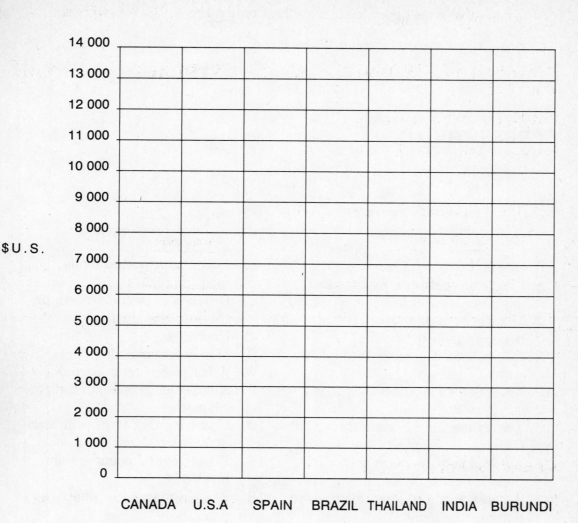

$U.S.

14 000
13 000
12 000
11 000
10 000
9 000
8 000
7 000
6 000
5 000
4 000
3 000
2 000
1 000
0

CANADA   U.S.A   SPAIN   BRAZIL   THAILAND   INDIA   BURUNDI

3. Foreign aid is _____. The Canadian government *p. 27*

sends its aid through an agency called _____. There

are also private agencies that send aid, such as _____,

_____, _____, and

_____.

4. What reasons can you suggest why Canadians should be involved in foreign
aid to the poor countries of the world?

(a) _____

(b) _____

(c) _____

p. 28

5. What value would events such as the Commonwealth Games have for Canada and the other countries involved? _____

_____

_____

VOCABULARY CROSSWORD

Clues

ACROSS

3. Goods

5. Difference between exports and imports

7. Moving from one form of transportation to another

8. Goods moved in large boxes (two words)

12. The value of a country's goods and services

16. The Prime _____ goes through Greenwich, England.

18. An item sent to another country

20. Canada has to _____ oranges.

21. An area that has some features that are the same

22. A _____ graph is used to show the population of several countries.

23. Items that are made (two words)

25. The number of people

26. The shape as seen from the side

28. To exchange

29. 40°W is a line of _____ .

30. Opposite of trade deficit (two words)

DOWN

1. Goods transported by air, ship, road, or rail

2. Distance in degrees north or south of the equator

4. Unprocessed

6. Money for investing

7. A tax placed on imported goods

9. Number of people per square kilometre

10. Countries that trade with each other (two words)

11. When several countries are involved

13. The counting of a country's population

14. Where many people live in a small area

15. When the value of imports is greater than the value of exports (two words)

17. An item brought in from another country

19. The easiest way of showing scale on a map

22. A graph using columns

24. Population density in the Arctic

27. Trade without tariffs is called _____ trade.

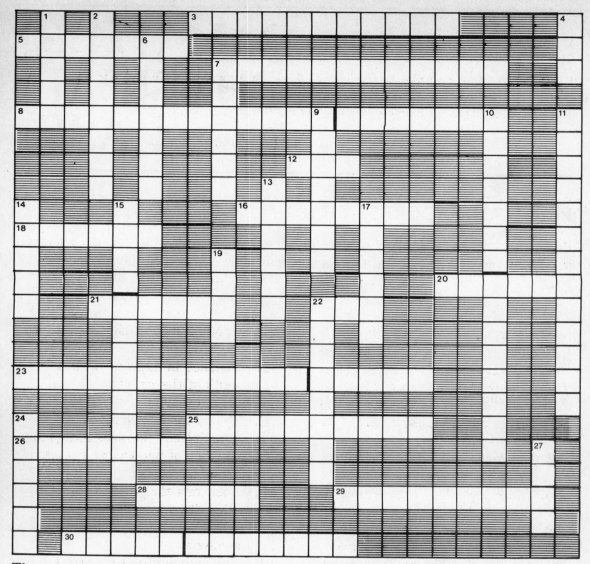

The answers are in the vocabulary on page 29 of the textbook and in Chapter 1.

2

CANADA'S PHYSICAL BASE

PERSONAL PROGRESS CHART

Put a check mark in the first square for each section when your teacher assigns it. When you have completed the section, put a check mark in the second square.

Page	Topic	Assigned by teacher	Completed by you
25	Landscape	☐	☐
28	How the Rock Structure Was Created	☐	☐
29	Weathering and Erosion	☐	☐
	Introduction to Mapping: Maps of Canada's Regions		
34	A. British Columbia	☐	☐
35	B. The Prairie Provinces	☐	☐
36	C. Ontario and Quebec	☐	☐
37	D. The Atlantic Provinces	☐	☐
38	E. Canada's Northern Territories	☐	☐
	Making and Reading Maps:		
39	Scale	☐	☐
42	Direction	☐	☐
43	Topographic Maps	☐	☐
47	Contour Lines	☐	☐
48	Mapping Exercises	☐	☐
56	Climate	☐	☐

59	Using Climatic Data _____	☐	☐
64	The Factors That Determine Climate ___	☐	☐
64	Latitude _____	☐	☐
66	Wind Direction and the Presence of Water Bodies _____	☐	☐
67	Mountain Ranges and Altitude _____	☐	☐
68	Ocean Currents _____	☐	☐
68	Precipitation _____	☐	☐
69	Orographic Precipitation _____	☐	☐
70	Convectional Precipitation _____	☐	☐
70	Cyclonic Precipitation _____	☐	☐
72	Weather Maps _____	☐	☐
73	Distribution of Precipitation in Canada ___	☐	☐
74	Vegetation, Soils, and Animals _____	☐	☐
75	Vegetation _____	☐	☐
80	Soil _____	☐	☐
83	Animals _____	☐	☐
85	Patterns of Wildlife _____	☐	☐
86	Extinction of Animals _____	☐	☐
88	National and Provincial Parks _____	☐	☐
89	Terra Nova National Park _____	☐	☐
91	Vocabulary Crossword _____	☐	☐

LANDSCAPE

1. Fill in the blanks.

p. 31

The two groups of forces that determine the shape of the land are

(a) _____

(b) _____

The Rock Foundation

Label the diagram from Figure 2-2.

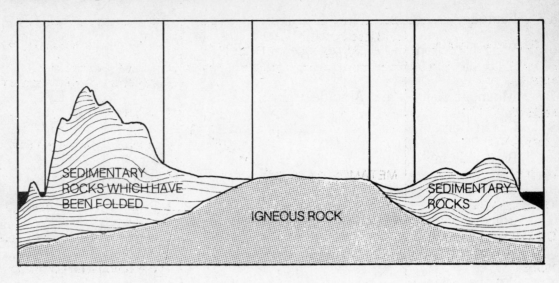

SEDIMENTARY
ROCKS WHICH HAVE
BEEN FOLDED

IGNEOUS ROCK

SEDIMENTARY
ROCKS

The Rock Cycle

p. 33

Label the diagram from Figure 2-8.

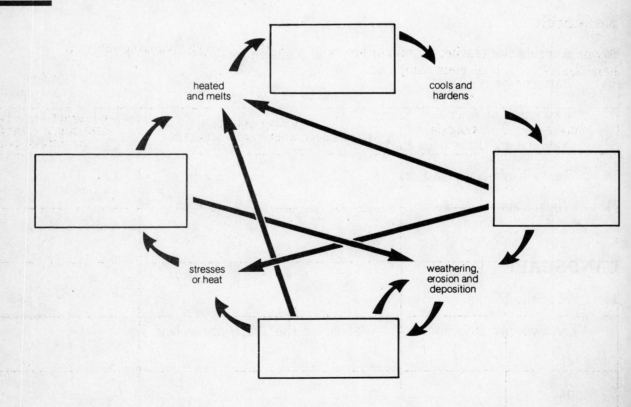

heated
and melts

cools and
hardens

stresses
or heat

weathering,
erosion and
deposition

2. Each of the following scrambled words is written in colour in the textbook on pages 32 to 33. Unscramble each word, and then use an arrow to connect it to the correct meaning.

pp. 32-33

Scrambled Words	Unscrambled Words	Arrows	Meanings
NSSEGI			Rock formed when magma cools
MIDESTNERYA			A "changed" rock
LSSOSIF			One type of metamorphic rock
HATMEPROCIM	METAMORPHIC		A rock made of layers
TSASNDOEN			Animals or plants preserved in rock
OISERON			One type of sedimentary rock
NGIEUOS			The wearing away of rocks
EHTAWERNIG			The breaking and rotting of rocks
NITGRAE			Molten rock
MMAGA			One igneous rock

Research

Arrange with your teacher to obtain ten rock samples. Use the following table to help describe each of your samples.

SAMPLE #	COLOUR	OTHER INFORMATION (GRITTINESS, WEIGHT, FOSSILS, ETC.)	PROBABLE ROCK FAMILY (IGNEOUS, SEDIMENTARY, OR METAMORPHIC

HOW THE ROCK STRUCTURE WAS CREATED

pp. 34-35

Here is a series of sketches that represents the stages in the formation of Canada's rock structure. After reading pages 34 to 35 in the textbook, write a short description of what is happening in each picture.

1. _____

2. _____

3. _____

4. _____

5. _____

6. _____

7. _____

QUIZ on Rocks and Rock Structure

Answer by circling T (True) or F (False).

1. The Western Mountains are mainly sedimentary rocks.   T   F
2. The Canadian Shield has the oldest Canadian rocks.   T   F
3. The Appalachian Mountains formed after the Western Mountains.   T   F
4. Weathering is the wearing away of rocks.   T   F
5. Sedimentary rocks usually form under the sea.   T   F
6. Metamorphic rocks can be found in the Canadian Shield.   T   F
7. The Appalachians are no longer being worn down.   T   F
8. Rocks on the top of fold mountains may contain seashell fossils.   T   F
9. The Innuitian Mountains formed at the same time as the
   Western Mountains.   T   F
10. Sedimentary rocks underlie the Interior Plains and Great Lakes–
    St. Lawrence Lowlands.   T   F

WEATHERING AND EROSION

Look at each of the photographs on pages 36 to 38 of the textbook and answer these questions.   *pp. 36-38*

Figure 2-12 _____

1. Write the title of the picture on the line above.

2. What colour is the water? _____

3. Where would the mud come from? _____

   _____

4. In which season was the picture probably

   taken? _____ Why do you

   say this? _____

   _____

Figure 2-13 _____

5. Write the title of the picture on the line above.

6. What caused the rock to break up into such *angular* pieces

   (ones with sharp corners and straight sides)? _____

   _____

   _____

Figure 2-14 _____

7. Write the title of the picture on the line above.

8. What force brought the broken rocks to the base of the cliff? _____

9. What animal is in the picture? _____
Circle it on this picture.

Figure 2-15 _____

10. Write the title of the picture on the line above.

11. Look carefully at the picture. Draw a line across where the soil surface used to be.

12. The tree was cut down before wind erosion started. How can you tell that this is true? _____

_____

Figure 2-16 _____

13. Write the title of the picture on the line above.

14. What are glaciers made from? _____

15. Explain why there are layers in the ice. _____

_____

_____

Figure 2-17 _____

16. Write the title of the picture on the line above.

17. The rocks in the mountains on the left are sedimentary. How can you tell this? _____

_____

_____

18. Give two reasons why few trees are growing on the mountain slopes.

(a) _____

(b) _____

Figure 2-18 _____

19. Write the title of the picture on the line above.

20. List two ways in which this picture differs from Figure 2-17.

    (a) _____

    (b) _____

Figure 2-19 _____

21. Write the title of the picture on the line above.

22. Label the following features on the photograph (use arrows).

woodland      orchard

farmland   buildings

road

Figure 2-20 _____

23. Write the title of the picture on the line above.

24. Circle the conditions that would lead to most erosion by waves.

soft cliffs      hard cliffs

high waves   small waves

offshore winds   onshore winds

gentle breezes   storm conditions

25. What is the building in the background? _____

_____

26. Look at each of the nine pictures referred to in questions 1 to 25 and shown on pages 36 to 38 of the textbook. Which kinds of scenery, shown in the photographs, have you seen? List these places and explain where you have seen each one.

SCENERY	I HAVE SEEN THIS AT . . .

The Major Processes of Landscape Formation

p. 38

Fill in the diagram from Figure 2-21 on page 38 of the textbook.

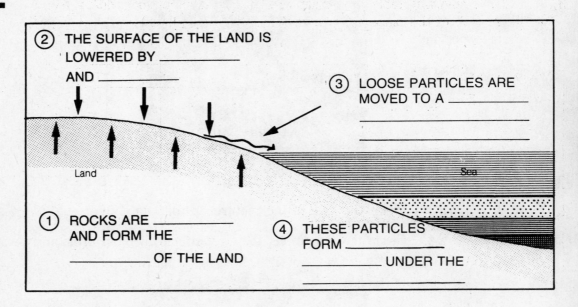

② THE SURFACE OF THE LAND IS LOWERED BY _____ AND _____

③ LOOSE PARTICLES ARE MOVED TO A _____ _____ _____

Land

Sea

① ROCKS ARE _____ AND FORM THE _____ OF THE LAND

④ THESE PARTICLES FORM _____ _____ UNDER THE _____

Research

Using encyclopedias or other books, fill in this chart.

NATURE'S ANGER

TOPIC (WRITE IN ONE EXAMPLE OF EACH)	YEAR OF OCCURRENCE	DESTRUCTION AND LOSS OF LIFE THAT RESULTED
Volcano (volcanic eruption)		

Earthquake		

The Hare's Vacation

Imagine that the Arctic hare, which you should be able to spot in Figure 2-14 on page 36, has decided that he wants to see the rest of Canada. *p. 36*

1. Give a suitable name to the hare. _____

2. Give two reasons why you think he might not be content to live in his home area.

   (a) _____

   (b) _____

3. Use the following table to explain what the hare might *like* and/or *dislike* about each of the places shown in the photographs listed.

FIGURE	PAGE	THE HARE WOULD LIKE:	THE HARE WOULD NOT LIKE:
2-12	36		
2-15	36		
2-16	37		
2-17	37		
2-18	37		

INTRODUCTION TO MAPPING: MAPS OF CANADA'S REGIONS

A. British Columbia

1. Write in "British Columbia" as a title.
2. Use a bright colour (like red) to show British Columbia *on the small map* of Canada.
3. Using your atlas as a guide, shade in and name British Columbia, and the province, territories, and country that border it. Use a different colour for each of the following: Yukon Territory, Northwest Territories, Alberta, continental U.S.A., Alaska.
4. With the help of an atlas, and using a blue pencil, lightly shade in the sea off the west coast.
5. Label the following bodies of water: Pacific Ocean, Dixon Entrance, Hecate Strait, Queen Charlotte Strait, Strait of Georgia, Juan de Fuca Strait.
6. Label the following physical features: Queen Charlotte Islands, Vancouver Island, Coast Mountains, Columbia Mountains, Rocky Mountains, Interior Plateau (east of the Coast Mountains), Interior Plains (in the northeast corner).
7. Label these important rivers: Fraser, Peace, Columbia. Write the names along the lines representing the rivers.
8. A *mountain pass* is a low point in a line or range of mountains. Label the three that are marked with arrows.
9. Name the cities and towns represented by dots on the map. Only some have their initials written in.

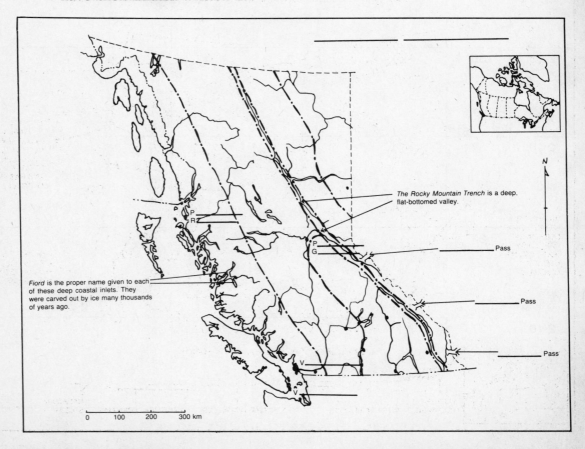

B. The Prairie Provinces

1. Write in "Prairie Provinces" as a title.
2. Use a bright colour (like red) to shade in the Prairie Provinces *on the small map* of Canada.
3. Using your atlas as a guide, shade in and name the following provinces, territories, and country where they touch the Prairie Provinces: Northwest Territories, British Columbia, Ontario, the U.S.A. Use a different colour for each.
4. Name Alberta, Saskatchewan, and Manitoba, with the help of an atlas. Using a blue pencil, lightly shade in the water off the northeast coast. Also shade in the lakes outlined on the map.
5. Label Hudson Bay and the following lakes: Athabasca, Wollaston, Reindeer, Winnipegosis, Manitoba, Winnipeg, Diefenbaker.
6. Label the following physical features: Western Mountains, Interior Plains, Canadian Shield. Also name Caribou Mountains, Swan Hills, Cypress Hills. *Note:* The boundaries between the physical features are represented by .— · —— · —.)
7. On the map, label these important rivers: Peace, Athabasca, Slave, Churchill, Nelson, North Saskatchewan, South Saskatchewan, Saskatchewan, Assiniboine, Red.
8. Name the five cities located where there are letters on the map.

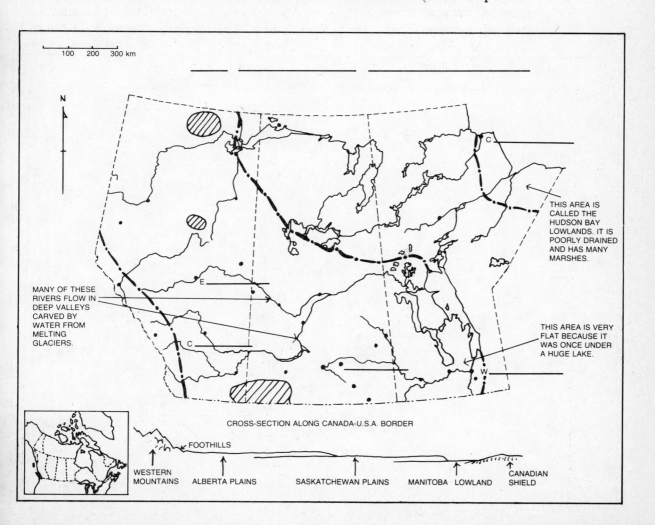

THIS AREA IS CALLED THE HUDSON BAY LOWLANDS. IT IS POORLY DRAINED AND HAS MANY MARSHES.

MANY OF THESE RIVERS FLOW IN DEEP VALLEYS CARVED BY WATER FROM MELTING GLACIERS.

THIS AREA IS VERY FLAT BECAUSE IT WAS ONCE UNDER A HUGE LAKE.

CROSS-SECTION ALONG CANADA-U.S.A. BORDER

FOOTHILLS

WESTERN MOUNTAINS   ALBERTA PLAINS   SASKATCHEWAN PLAINS   MANITOBA LOWLAND   CANADIAN SHIELD

C. Ontario and Quebec

1. Write in "Ontario and Quebec" as a title.
2. Use a bright colour (like red) to show Ontario and Quebec *on the small map* of Canada.
3. Using your atlas as a guide, shade in and label the following provinces, territories, and country that border this region: Manitoba, Newfoundland (Labrador), New Brunswick, U.S.A. Label Ontario and Quebec.
4. With the help of an atlas and using a blue pencil, lightly shade in the ocean and the major lakes.
5. Label these parts of the ocean: Hudson Bay, James Bay, Hudson Strait, Ungava Bay, Gulf of St. Lawrence.
6. Label these lakes: Superior, Michigan, Huron, Erie, Ontario, Nipigon, Lake-of-the-Woods, Lac St-Jean.
7. Label the area of the Canadian Shield, the Great Lakes–St. Lawrence Lowlands (the two arrows point to this small area), and the Hudson Bay Lowlands.
8. Name these islands: Belcher, Ile Anticosti, Akimiski, Manitoulin. Label also the Gaspé Peninsula.
9. Label these important rivers: St. Lawrence, Ottawa, La Grande Rivière, Moose, Attawapiskat, Severn, Albany.
10. Name these settlements: Toronto, Montreal, Hamilton, St. Catharines, London, Windsor, Sudbury, Sault Ste. Marie, Thunder Bay, Moosonee, Ottawa, Quebec, Chicoutimi, Fort Chimo, Kapuskasing, Timmins, Kenora.

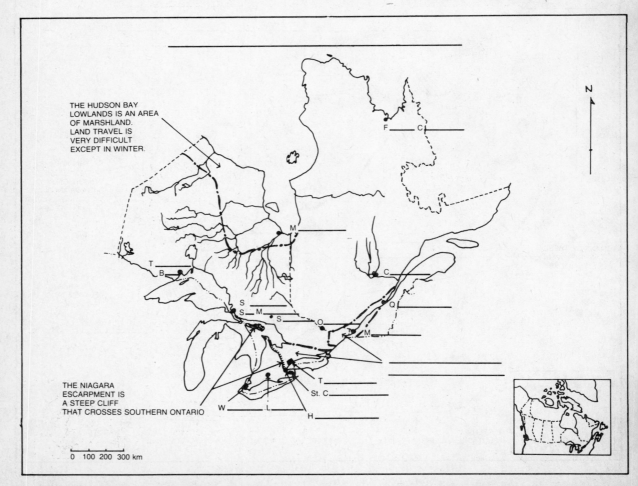

THE HUDSON BAY LOWLANDS IS AN AREA OF MARSHLAND. LAND TRAVEL IS VERY DIFFICULT EXCEPT IN WINTER.

THE NIAGARA ESCARPMENT IS A STEEP CLIFF THAT CROSSES SOUTHERN ONTARIO

0 100 200 300 km

D. The Atlantic Provinces

1. Write in "Atlantic Provinces" as a title.
2. Use a bright colour (like red) to show the Atlantic Provinces *on the small map* of Canada.
3. Using your atlas as a guide, shade in and label Quebec and the U.S.A. where each touches the Atlantic Provinces. Use different colours for Quebec and the U.S.A.
4. Label Newfoundland, Labrador (Newfoundland), New Brunswick, Prince Edward Island, and Nova Scotia.
5. With the help of an atlas and using a blue pencil, lightly shade in the ocean.
6. Label the following parts of the ocean: Davis Strait, Atlantic Ocean, Gulf of St. Lawrence, Cabot Strait, Northumberland Strait, Bay of Fundy, Strait of Belle Isle.
7. Use a brown pencil to shade in those areas that are above 300 m. In your atlas these areas are a lighter green than the lower areas, or possibly brown.
8. In Newfoundland, label the Long Range Mountains and Central Plateau. In Nova Scotia, label the Cape Breton Highlands and Nova Scotia Uplands. In New Brunswick, label the Central Uplands.
9. Label these important lakes: Lobstick Lake, Lake Melville, Grand Lake (Newfoundland), Bras d'Or Lake, Grand Lake (New Brunswick).
10. Label these rivers: Churchill, Exploits, Saint John.
11. Label the 14 cities or towns located where there are letters on the map.

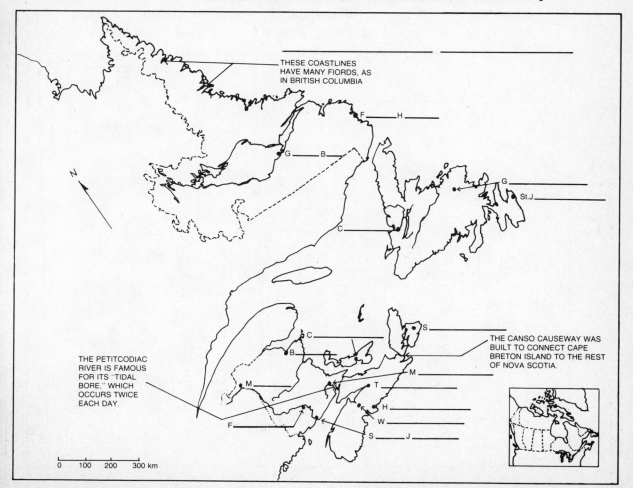

THESE COASTLINES HAVE MANY FIORDS, AS IN BRITISH COLUMBIA

St.J

THE CANSO CAUSEWAY WAS BUILT TO CONNECT CAPE BRETON ISLAND TO THE REST OF NOVA SCOTIA.

THE PETITCODIAC RIVER IS FAMOUS FOR ITS "TIDAL BORE," WHICH OCCURS TWICE EACH DAY.

0   100   200   300 km

E. Canada's Northern Territories

1. Write in "Canada's Northern Territories" as a title.
2. Use a bright colour (like red) to show the two Northern Territories *on the small map* of Canada.
3. Using your atlas as a guide, shade in and label the provinces and the U.S.A. where they border the territories. Use a different colour for each of the following: Alaska (U.S.A.), British Columbia, Alberta, Saskatchewan, Manitoba.
4. Label the Yukon Territory, the Northwest Territories, and the three districts that make up the Northwest Territories (Franklin, Mackenzie, and Keewatin).
5. With the help of an atlas and using a blue pencil, lightly shade in the ocean around the mainland coast and around the islands.
6. Label the following parts of the ocean: Hudson Bay, Detroit d'Hudson, Foxe Basin, Baffin Bay, Lancaster Sound, and Viscount Melville Sound.
7. Label these major lakes: Great Bear, Great Slave. (Remember: Great Slave Lake has an *S* to start *Slave* and is *south* of Great Bear Lake.)
8. On the mainland (not the islands) colour in lightly and name: Western Mountains, Interior Plains, Canadian Shield. The boundary between these regions is ·—·—·—· .
9. Label these islands: Baffin, Ellesmere, Queen Elizabeth Islands, and Victoria Island.
10. Label these important rivers: Mackenzie, Yukon.
11. Label these settlements: Whitehorse, Yellowknife, Dawson, Aklavik, Inuvik, Coppermine, Pine Point, Rankin Inlet, Iqaluit, Resolute, Alert.

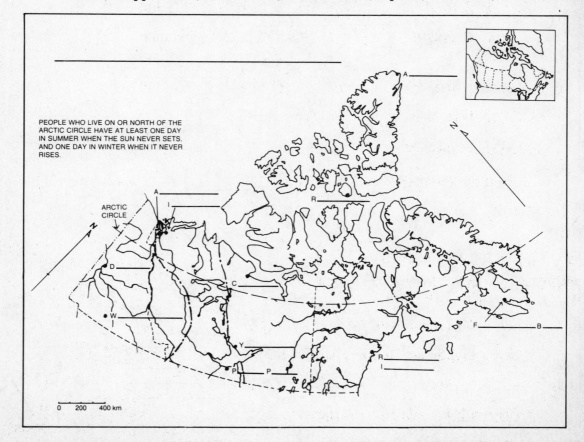

PEOPLE WHO LIVE ON OR NORTH OF THE ARCTIC CIRCLE HAVE AT LEAST ONE DAY IN SUMMER WHEN THE SUN NEVER SETS, AND ONE DAY IN WINTER WHEN IT NEVER RISES.

ARCTIC CIRCLE

0   200   400 km

MAKING AND READING MAPS: SCALE

1. What is scale? _____ *p. 39*
2. Read about the three ways of explaining scale (pages 39 and 40 in the textbook). Summarize the information on this chart.

SCALE TYPE	EXAMPLE	EQUIPMENT NEEDED	ADVANTAGES/DISADVANTAGES
Line		Paper or string	
			Simple to calculate distances
	1:50 000		

3. Answer questions 8, 9, 10, 11 on pages 39 and 40 of the textbook. Put your answers in the spaces below. *pp. 39-40*

    (8) **(a)** A to B is _____ km   **(c)** A to C is _____ km

        (b) B to C is _____ km   **(d)** The total distance ABCD is _____ km

    (9) **(a)** E to F is _____ km   **(c)** E to H is _____ km

        (b) G to H is _____ km   **(d)** The total distance EGF is _____ km

    (10) **(a)** J to K is _____ km   **(c)** N to K is _____ km

        (b) L to M is _____ km

    (11) I think that the _____ scale is the easiest

        one to use because _____

        _____ .

4. **(a)** Using this line scale:

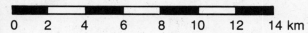

What is the straight-line distance between

• Ned's Lighthouse and Dolphin Point?

    _____ km

• Dolphin Point and Haida's Harbour via

Treasure Hill? _____ km

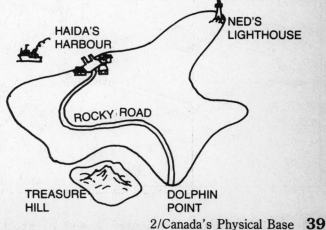

(b) Using the same line scale, what is the distance from Haida's Harbour to Dolphin Point along Rocky Road? (Use a piece of string.) _____ km

(c) Which is the shortest boat route from Haida's Harbour to Dolphin Point? _____

Measure each of the three possible routes and then colour in the shortest on the map. Write the distance here. _____ km

(d) If the scale of the map were 1 cm rep 30 km, calculate these two distances:

- The straight-line distance from Haida's Harbour to the lighthouse _____ km

- Treasure Hill to Ned's Lighthouse _____ km

p. 41   **5.** Large- and Small-Scale Maps

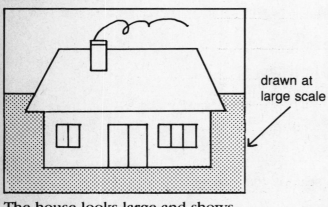

drawn at
large scale

The house looks large and shows much detail, but only of one object.

drawn at
a smaller scale

The house looks small with little detail, but the picture includes a much larger area.

LARGE-SCALE MAP

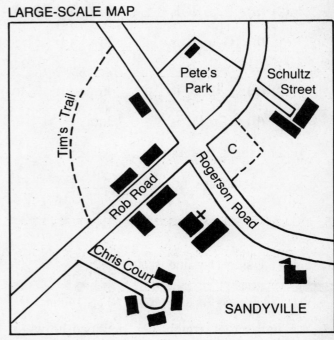

SMALL-SCALE MAP

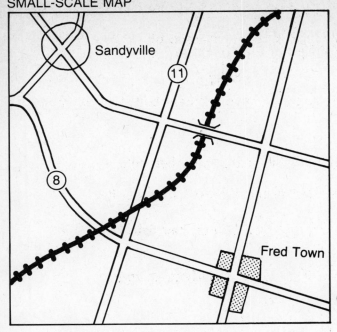

Sandyville

11

8

Fred Town

(a) Look at the two maps above.
Fill in the table, answering yes or no.

CAN YOU SEE:	LARGE-SCALE MAP	SMALL-SCALE MAP
Individual houses		
Names of small roads		
Types of buildings		
Major routes		
Nearest other town		

(b) What would be the main uses for the large-scale map? _____

_____

What would be the main uses for the small-scale map? _____

_____

(c) A map that shows much detail of a small area is a _____ - scale map.

A map that shows little detail but covers a large area is a _____

- scale map.

DIRECTION

p. 42.

1.

2. With the help of your teacher, draw an arrow in the box on the right, showing where north is in your classroom.

Write in the names and initials of the eight points of the compass.

FRONT

3. **(a)** Follow the instructions to this pattern puzzle. The first few moves are shown. See what pattern you make by tracing the route. Put your pencil on START. Draw a line following these directions:
2 squares NE, 1 E, 1 N,
1 E, 1 S, 1 E, 2 S,
1 W, 2 S, 2 W, 1 N,
1 W, 1 S, 2 W, 2 N,
1 W.

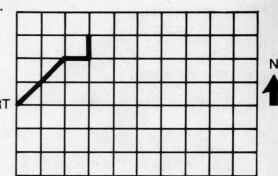

The object is a _____ .

(b) Make up your own pattern puzzle by writing the directions below. Use a piece of tracing paper over the grid. Challenge somebody to find out the shape. (Make sure you hide the answer.)

_____   _____

_____   _____

_____   _____

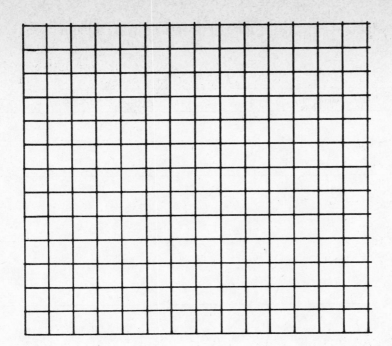

(c) TREASURE HUNT

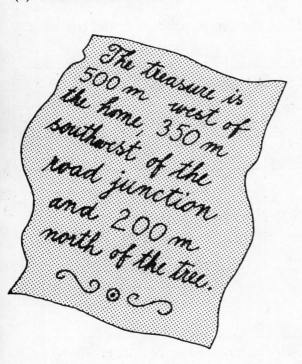

The treasure is 500 m west of the home, 350 m southeast of the road junction and 200 m north of the tree.

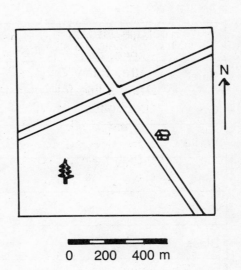

0   200   400 m

Where would you dig for the treasure?

TOPOGRAPHIC MAPS

1. What are topographic maps? _____ *p. 42*

_____

What kinds of information do they show? _____

_____

2/Canada's Physical Base **43**

2. Use this table to answer question 14 at the top of page 44 in the textbook.

OBJECT IN PHOTOGRAPH	WHAT IT LOOKS LIKE
Lake	
Trees	
Fields	
Roads	

3. Use this table to answer question 15 at the top of page 44 in the textbook.

COLOUR USED ON TOPOGRAPHIC MAPS:	THIS COLOUR IS USED TO SHOW:
Blue	
Green	
White	
Red	
Pink	
Black	
Orange	

4. A map symbol is _____ .

Symbols and their meanings are shown in a _____ or

_____ on the map.

Fill in the symbols that are shown on page 44 of the textbook. A few extra boxes are included so that you can put in some additional symbols from the key or legend of a topographic map supplied by your teacher.

☐ House   ☐ Power transmission line

☐ Church   ☐ Telephone line

☐ School   ☐ Mine

☐ Post office   ☐ Airport

☐ Greenhouse   ☐ Swamp

☐ R.C.M.P. post   ☐ Bridge

☐ Tower   ☐ River

☐ Single-track railway   ☐ Docks

☐ Seaplane base   ☐ Cemetery

☐   ☐

☐   ☐

5. Look at the map on page 43. Copy each of the symbols used on the map. Beside each of your symbols, write down what the symbol means. (Are you able to see a lake, forests, river, road, post office, church, and bridge?) Try to suggest what the dotted line might mean.

p. 43

I think that the dotted line represents _____ .

6. Answer question 17 from page 44 of the textbook.

p. 44

(a) I consider the photograph to be more useful than the map for _____

_____

_____

_____ .

(b) The map is more useful than the photograph for _____

_____

_____ .

(c) Fill in the table.

JOBS USING MAPS OR PHOTOGRAPHS	HOW THEY WOULD BE USED

(d) Air photographs and topographic maps have benefited people in the following ways:

_____

_____

_____

_____

pp. 44-45

7. The military grid is shown as a _____ grid on

topographic maps. These lines are used for _____ on a

map.

8. Answer questions 18 and 19 at the bottom of page 44 of the textbook.

(18) The military grid co-ordinates for D are _____ .

The military grid co-ordinates for E are _____ .

(19) It is important for the army to describe locations accurately because

_____ .

9. Answer questions 20 and 21 from page 45 of the textbook.

(20) The church is at grid reference _____ .

The school is at grid reference _____ .

(21) At 485692 the symbol is _____ , which means_____.

At 488708 the symbol is _____ , which means_____.

At 472702 the symbol is _____ , which means_____.

10.

Put in the following symbols at the places indicated.

A school at 230400

A house at 244400

A bridge at 230415 (Make the bridge

go north to south.)

A mine at 230425

A tower at 241420

Use a pencil to make this route on the grid above:

Rosemary left school and crossed the bridge on her way to the mine. She then walked to the tower, which she climbed before crossing the bridge again. She finally went home, one hour late!

What letter of the alphabet have you drawn? _____

CONTOUR LINES

1. A contour line joins points that have _____ . They are

   shown as _____ lines on topographic maps. The
   (colour)

   contour _____ is the height difference between

   adjacent (next-door) contours.

   p. 45

2. Answer questions 22 to 25 from page 46 of the textbook.

   p. 46

   (22) The contour interval of the map (b) on page 47 is _____.

   (23) **(a)** There are _____ contour lines on the flat arm of land.

   (b) The contour lines _____ where there

   are steep slopes.

   (24) **(a)** When contour lines on a map are close together, _____

   _____ .

(b) When contour lines on a map are far apart, _____ .

(25) When contour lines cross a valley, they _____

_____ .

MAPPING EXERCISES

Making a Model

You are going to make a model from this map. You will need a *piece of cardboard* to make the base. It should be the same size as this rectangle. You will need small pieces of construction paper or coloured cards, preferably blue, green, yellow, and brown. In addition you should have carbon paper, scissors, glue, and normal writing materials.

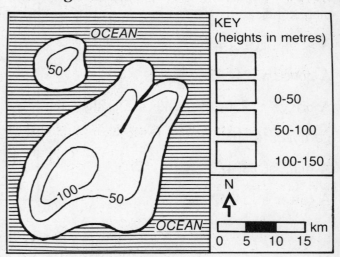

These are the steps you should follow.

1. Carefully cut your piece of cardboard to the size of the map. It should be large enough to hold the ocean and the key and scale.
2. Cut out a smaller rectangle from your blue construction paper to cover the area of the ocean, including the two islands.
3. **(a)** Slip your green construction paper under this page.
    (b) Place your carbon paper under this page but on top of your construction paper.
    (c) Press heavily and draw the outline of the two islands.
    (d) Cut out the two islands and glue them onto the blue ocean in the correct positions.
4. **(a)** Using carbon paper and the yellow construction paper, trace the 50-m contour lines.
    (b) Cut out the 50-m outline and glue it on top of the green islands you already have.
5. Using carbon paper and your brown construction paper, repeat your tracing for the 100-m outline and glue the brown paper on top. You now have your 3-layer contour map of the islands.
6. **(a)** Draw in the stream, as shown.
    (b) Draw in your key, using portions of your coloured construction paper.
    (c) Include a north arrow and a scale.

YOUR MODEL IS COMPLETE!

Contour Map

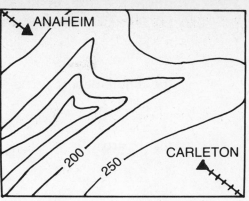

1. Finish numbering the contour lines.
2. Circle the steepest slope and write ''steep'' across that portion of the map.
3. Draw in two streams that join into a larger stream.
4. Mark the best route for a railway between Anaheim and Carleton. Avoid any steep slopes.

Maps from the Six Regions of Canada

1. Write your answers beside the questions.

p. 47

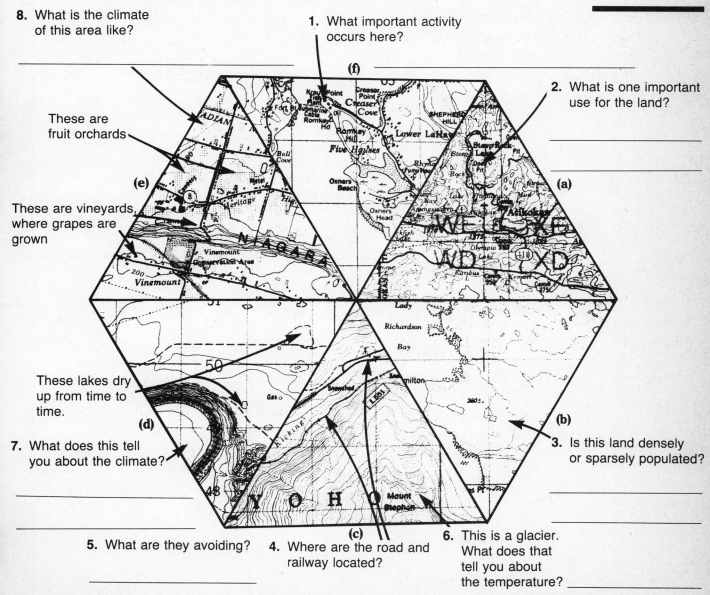

8. What is the climate of this area like?

1. What important activity occurs here?

2. What is one important use for the land?

These are fruit orchards

These are vineyards, where grapes are grown

These lakes dry up from time to time.

7. What does this tell you about the climate?

3. Is this land densely or sparsely populated?

5. What are they avoiding?

4. Where are the road and railway located?

6. This is a glacier. What does that tell you about the temperature?

2. Answer questions 27 and 28 from pages 47 and 48 in the textbook.

(27) **(a)** The flattest areas are shown in maps ＿＿＿＿＿＿＿＿＿＿ and

＿＿＿＿＿＿＿＿＿＿ .

(b) The steepest areas are shown in maps ＿＿＿＿＿＿＿＿＿＿ and

＿＿＿＿＿＿＿＿＿＿ .

(c) In area ＿＿＿＿＿＿＿＿＿ the land is ＿＿＿＿＿＿＿＿＿

＿＿＿＿＿＿＿＿＿＿＿＿＿＿＿＿＿＿＿＿＿＿＿＿ .

The vegetation is ＿＿＿＿＿＿＿＿＿＿＿＿＿＿＿＿＿＿ .

In area ＿＿＿＿＿＿＿＿＿ the land is ＿＿＿＿＿＿＿＿＿

＿＿＿＿＿＿＿＿＿＿＿＿＿＿＿＿＿＿＿＿＿＿＿＿ .

The vegetation is ＿＿＿＿＿＿＿＿＿＿＿＿＿＿＿＿＿＿ .

(d) People could make use of the land in ＿＿＿＿＿＿＿＿＿

＿＿＿＿＿＿＿＿＿＿＿＿＿＿＿＿＿＿＿＿＿＿＿＿＿

＿＿＿＿＿＿＿＿＿＿＿＿＿＿＿＿＿＿＿＿＿＿＿＿＿

and in ＿＿＿＿＿＿＿＿＿ by ＿＿＿＿＿＿＿＿＿

＿＿＿＿＿＿＿＿＿＿＿＿＿＿＿＿＿＿＿＿＿＿＿＿ .

(e) I would most like to live in area ＿＿＿＿＿＿＿＿＿＿

because ＿＿＿＿＿＿＿＿＿＿＿＿＿＿＿＿＿＿＿＿＿

＿＿＿＿＿＿＿＿＿＿＿＿＿＿＿＿＿＿＿＿＿＿＿＿＿

＿＿＿＿＿＿＿＿＿＿＿＿＿＿＿＿＿＿＿＿＿＿＿＿ .

I would least like to live in area ＿＿＿＿＿＿＿＿＿＿

because ＿＿＿＿＿＿＿＿＿＿＿＿＿＿＿＿＿＿＿＿＿

＿＿＿＿＿＿＿＿＿＿＿＿＿＿＿＿＿＿＿＿＿＿＿＿＿

＿＿＿＿＿＿＿＿＿＿＿＿＿＿＿＿＿＿＿＿＿＿＿＿ .

(28) Fill in the details in the blank boxes.

REGION	LETTER	TWO REASONS
Western Mountains	C	Steep, ice in high parts
Interior Plains		
Canadian Shield		
Great Lakes–St. Lawrence Lowlands		
Appalachian Mountains		
Arctic		

Profiles

p. 48

After you have read the section explaining how to make profiles from contour maps, work on the following ones.

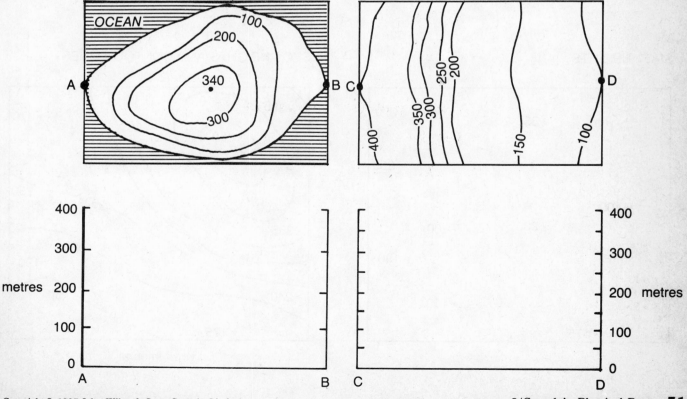

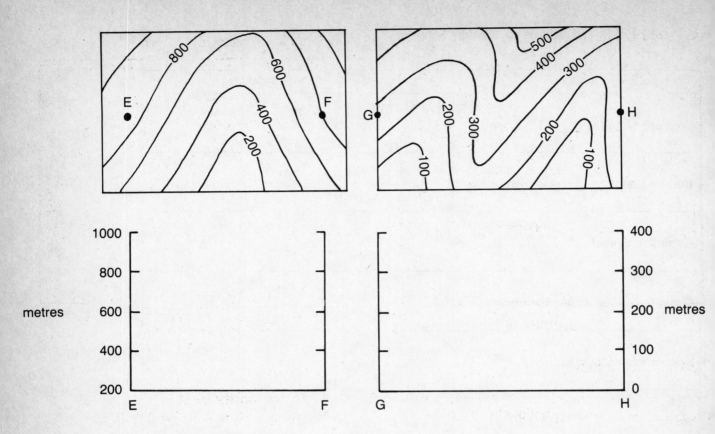

metres

A Dotty Challenge

Drawing a map with contour lines involves several steps. When the surveyor takes measurements of the land, he or she finds the positions and heights of several places. These spot heights are plotted in a map, as shown below. Contour lines at a selected interval are then plotted.

SPOT HEIGHTS

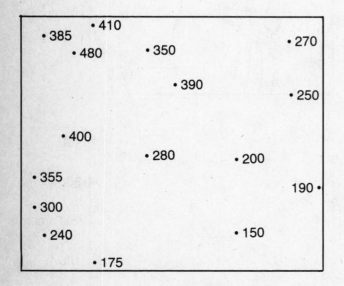

SPOT HEIGHTS AND CONTOUR LINES

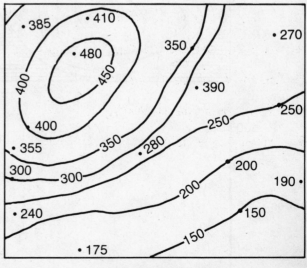

Contour interval 50 m

1. Complete this map.

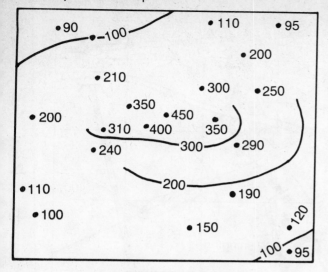

•90 •—100— •110 •95
•200
•210
•300 •250
•350
•450
•200
•310 •400 350
•240 —300— •290
—200—
•110 •190
•100
•150 •120
100 •95

Contour interval 100 m

2. Draw in the contours.

•540 •560 •610 •620
•500
•470
•510 •550
•450
•400 •430
•430
•350
•300 •360
•490 •400
•310 •320
•250
•470 •250
•300 •210
•510
•260
•380
•440 •420 •340

Contour interval 50 m

Saturday Spin

Look at page 44 in your textbook for a key to the symbols used on the next page. Follow the instructions and answer the questions as you go. Start at 467763.

Drive westwards along the road for 2 km.
Turn left.
Drive for 0.5 km.

1. What kind of building is on your left? _____

2. What is the name of the village you are in? _____

3. Is the train station on your left or right? _____

Turn right just after you pass the post office.

Drive along the road, keeping right where the road branches.

4. Are you driving uphill or downhill? _____

5. Is the slope gentle or steep? _____

6. What structure is at the end of the road? _____

7. What is the height of the base of this structure? _____

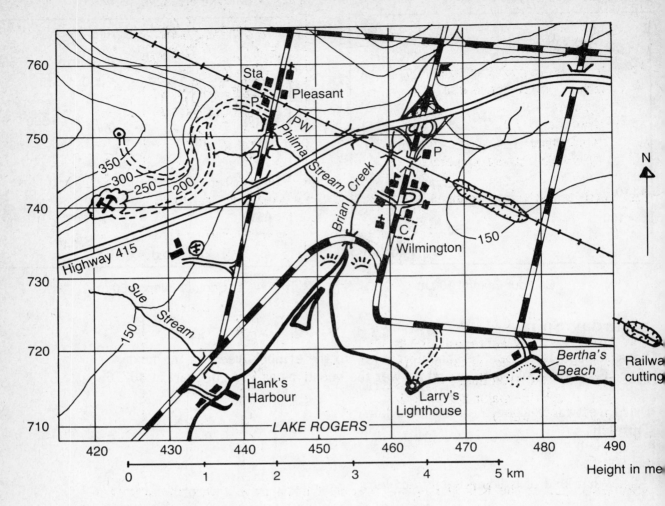

You climb to the top.

8. What can you see about a kilometre to the south? _____

You drive back along the road to the turn where the post office is, and turn

right.

9. What is the name of the stream you cross? _____

10. Do you drive under or over the highway? _____

Turn right 1 km south of the highway.

11. What is 0.5 km along this road? _____

You decide to go for a flight. After taking off, you turn south, and follow the

coastline toward the east. You fly over a harbour.

12. What is the name of the harbour? _____

13. What is the next tall building you see? _____

You turn north and look down on a village.

14. On the enlarged map to the left, mark in where there is a
    cemetery
    school
    post office
    (Use the correct symbols.)

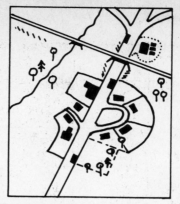

Just north of the village there is a complicated "cloverleaf" intersection.

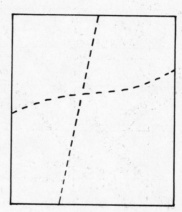

15. Draw the intersection as seen from the air in the space on the right. (The dotted lines will help you to get the major roads in the correct positions.)

After passing over the R.C.M.P. post, your pilot turns back toward the airport.

16. In which direction are you flying? Toward the _____

After landing safely you decide to go swimming, and drive to Bertha's Beach.

17. What is the grid reference for Bertha's Beach? _____

Late in the afternoon you drive back to your starting point.

18. How many kilometres is it by road from Bertha's Beach back to your starting point? _____ km

CLIMATE

p. 49

Weather is important to us all, but it is of vital importance to some.

1. Fill in this table.

OCCUPATION	IMPORTANCE OF WEATHER ON THE JOB	SPECIAL MEASURES TAKEN TO OVERCOME THESE PROBLEMS
Airline pilot		
Construction worker		
Firefighter		
Student		
Farmer		
Person who delivers home heating oil		
Bus driver		
Telephone line repairer		
Supermarket cashier		
Occupation of your choice		

pp. 49-50

2. Unscramble the words below to fill in the blanks, and then finish each sentence.

_____ is the layer of air that _____ .
    POTAMSHREE

_____ includes the _____ changes
    EWEHTAR

in _____ .

_____ is the _____
    LIMETAC

for a certain place taken over many _____ .

_____ includes _____ and
    TRPTIPCEIAION

_____ .

p. 51

3. After examining the map of climatic regions on page 51 of the textbook and the map given to you on page 57,

(a) Give the following map the title "The Climatic Regions of Canada."
(b) Carefully mark the boundaries of the six climatic regions of Canada. Name and colour in each of these regions.
(c) Fill in the blanks in the descriptions of each region.

TITLE: _____

MOUNTAIN REGION

Winter and summer conditions

_____ _____ in different parts

of the region. Valleys and southern

areas are generally _____ than

_____ and _____ areas.

Precipitation is also _____ .

Western slopes of mountains usually

receive _____ precipitation

than _____ slopes.

ARCTIC REGION

Winter is very _____ and lasts _____ to _____

months. Summer is _____ and _____ :

Precipitation is very _____ .

NORTHERN REGION

Winter is _____ and lasts _____

months. Summer is _____ and _____ .

Precipitation is _____ and

occurs mainly in the _____ .

PACIFIC REGION

Winter is _____ with

temperatures usually

_____ _____ .

Summer is _____ .

Precipitation is very

_____ and comes

mainly in the _____ .

PRAIRIE REGION

Winter is _____ .

Summer is _____ .

Precipitation is _____

and comes mainly

in the _____ .

SOUTHEASTERN REGION

Winter is _____

in _____ area.

Winter is _____

in the _____ .

Summer _____ .

Precipitation _____ .

4. **(a)** Look again at the map of climatic regions of Canada.
At each place marked, the top temperature is the lowest monthly temperature, which usually occurs in January. List the centre where each of the following winter temperatures is recorded.

-33°C _____   -12°C _____

-29°C _____   -12°C _____

-26°C _____   -11°C _____

-23°C _____   - 6°C _____

-20°C _____   - 3°C _____

-18°C _____   - 3°C _____

-15°C _____   - 2°C _____

-13°C _____   + 4°C _____

(b) Rank the 16 places according to summer temperatures, warmest first and coldest last.

°C   °C

____ _____   ____ _____

____ _____   ____ _____

____ _____   ____ _____

____ _____   ____ _____

____ _____   ____ _____

____ _____   ____ _____

____ _____   ____ _____

____ _____   ____ _____

p. 50

5. Study the map of precipitation on page 50 of the textbook. Fill in the blanks.

The wettest area of Canada extends in a narrow strip along the

_____ coast. The other wet areas are along the _____

coast and in some isolated areas of _____

_____ . The part of Canada that receives the least

precipitation is the central _____ .

Dry areas are found in much of the _____ mainland,

the _____ parts of Alberta and Saskatchewan, and

some parts of _____ _____. The

remaining areas of Canada have moderate precipitation.

USING CLIMATIC DATA

1. Read the description in the textbook of how weather information is collected and made into weather maps (pages 52 and 53). Answer these questions.

   pp. 52-53

   (a) At how many places in Canada are weather observations made?

   _____

   (b) What are each of the following instruments used to measure?

   Thermometer _____

   Radiosonde (carried by helium balloon) _____

   (c) Where is this information sent to? _____

   (d) In what form is the information sent? _____

   (e) What is drawn, using the information? _____

   (f) What do meteorologists use these for? _____

2. **(a)** The word that means "highest (temperature)" is _____ .

   p. 54

   (b) The word that means "lowest (temperature)" is _____ .

   (c) The range of temperature is the _____ .

3. **(a)** To find the range of temperature, you pick out the maximum and minimum temperatures. The first one is done for you as an example.

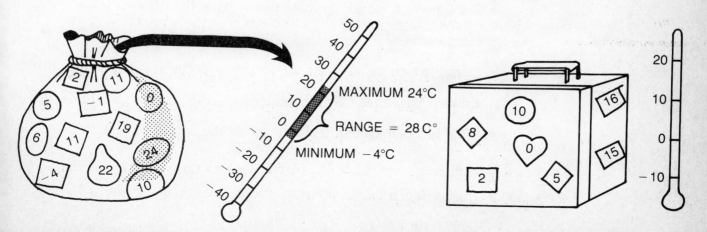

MAXIMUM 24°C

RANGE = 28 C°

MINIMUM −4°C

(b) If the maximum temperature is 15°C and the minimum is −5°C, what

is the range of temperature? _____ °C

If the maximum temperature is 22°C and the minimum is 2°C, what is

the range? _____ °C

pp. 54-55　　**4.** Figures of temperature and precipitation from many places in Canada are shown on pages 61 and 62 of this workbook and on pages 54 and 55 of the textbook. Figures are given for each month of the year. The last column shows the yearly average temperature and the total yearly precipitation.

(a) Looking at the yearly averages:

- What is the coldest place among those listed?

_____ (_____ °C)

- Which is the warmest place? _____

(_____ °C)

- Which is the driest among those listed? _____

(_____ mm precipitation)

- Which is the wettest place? _____

(_____ mm precipitation)

(b) Cut a piece of string, wool, or long paper to the length of the amount of precipitation in the wettest place.

Do the same for the place closest to where you live. How many

times wetter is it in the wettest

place? _____ times

(c) Circle the maximum and minimum temperatures for each place listed on pages 61 and 62 in the workbook.

- During which month do most places have their lowest

temperatures? _____

- During which month does the minimum occur in Nova Scotia, Prince

Edward Island, and Newfoundland? _____ .

- What is the minimum temperature in the centre closest to

you? _____ °C

- During which month do most places have their highest

temperatures? _____

　　　　　　　　Copyright © 1987 John Wiley & Sons Canada Limited

LOCATION		HEIGHT (m)	J	F	M	A	M	J	J	A	S	O	N	D	ANNUAL
Victoria (B.C.)	°C	69	2.9	4.7	5.8	8.6	11.9	14.5	16.4	16.1	13.9	10.0	6.2	4.2	9.6
	mm		146	97	69	44	30	29	18	25	37	87	128	146	856
Kamloops (B.C.)	°C	379	-6.0	-1.3	3.6	9.3	14.3	18.0	20.9	19.7	15.0	8.4	1.7	-2.6	8.4
	mm		29	16	8	12	19	36	26	27	20	18	21	28	260
Prince Rupert (B.C.)	°C	52	1.8	2.7	3.7	6.2	9.6	11.8	13.6	13.9	12.0	8.7	5.1	2.9	7.7
	mm		214	209	180	184	123	107	121	147	242	359	269	259	2414
Prince George (B.C.)	°C	676	-11.8	-6.2	-2.1	3.9	9.4	13.0	14.9	13.7	9.8	4.7	-2.8	-7.6	3.2
	mm		59	43	32	30	42	58	58	73	56	61	55	54	621
Edmonton (Alta.)	°C	1397	-14.7	-10.5	-5.4	4.0	10.0	14.7	17.5	15.9	10.9	5.4	-4.2	-10.7	2.8
	mm		25	20	17	23	37	75	83	72	36	18	18	21	445
Grande Prairie (Alta.)	°C	668	-17.3	-12.4	-7.4	2.4	10.0	13.7	16.0	14.8	10.2	4.2	-6.3	-13.2	1.2
	mm		34	28	21	22	38	64	60	53	34	26	31	30	441
Medicine Hat (Alta.)	°C	721	-12.1	-8.1	-3.2	5.9	12.1	16.1	20.2	18.9	13.2	7.6	-1.6	-7.6	5.1
	mm		23	18	19	25	38	64	39	39	33	17	16	16	347
Prince Albert (Sask.)	°C	431	-21.1	-16.9	-10.4	1.7	9.5	14.3	17.7	16.2	10.2	3.9	-7.1	-16.4	0.1
	mm		17	17	19	24	36	57	64	53	35	24	21	22	389
Regina (Sask.)	°C	574	-17.3	-14.3	-8.3	3.3	10.6	15.3	18.9	17.9	11.6	5.3	-5.2	-12.9	2.1
	mm		18	17	18	23	41	83	58	50	36	19	18	16	397
Saskatoon (Sask.)	°C	501	-18.7	-15.1	-8.7	3.3	10.6	15.4	18.8	17.4	11.3	5.0	-5.8	-14.0	1.6
	mm		18	18	17	21	34	57	53	45	33	19	19	18	352
The Pas (Man.)	°C	272	-22.4	-18.3	-11.4	0.4	7.7	14.0	17.9	16.3	10.2	3.8	-7.5	-17.4	-0.6
	mm		18	16	21	25	38	59	72	62	55	31	29	23	449
Winnipeg (Man.)	°C	240	-18.3	-15.7	-8.1	3.3	10.6	16.5	19.7	18.7	12.6	6.6	-4.4	-13.7	2.3
	mm		24	19	26	37	57	80	80	74	53	35	27	23	535
Kapuskasing (Ont.)	°C	229	-18.2	-15.8	-9.1	0.7	7.8	14.1	17.0	15.5	10.7	5.3	-4.1	-14.2	0.8
	mm		53	48	54	51	79	85	96	92	92	78	87	56	871
Ottawa (Ont.)	°C	126	-10.9	-9.5	-3.1	5.6	12.4	18.2	20.7	19.3	14.6	8.7	1.4	-7.7	5.8
	mm		60	57	61	68	70	73	81	82	79	66	78	77	852
Thunder Bay (Ont.)	°C	196	-14.8	-13.0	-6.2	2.4	8.3	13.8	17.5	16.5	11.3	6.1	-2.5	-10.8	2.4
	mm		48	30	44	56	75	83	71	88	84	57	57	46	739
Windsor (Ont.)	°C	194	-4.3	-3.4	1.2	8.2	14.0	19.9	22.3	21.3	17.4	11.6	4.3	-2.0	9.2
	mm		55	52	66	81	83	84	83	82	61	63	62	64	836

LOCATION	HEIGHT (m)		J	F	M	A	M	J	J	A	S	O	N	D	ANNUAL
Montreal (Que.)	57	°C	-8.9	-7.6	-1.4	6.7	13.6	19.1	21.6	20.4	15.8	10.1	2.9	-5.7	7.2
		mm	80	71	75	77	75	87	93	92	87	79	93	91	1000
Quebec City (Que.)	75	°C	-11.6	-10.6	-4.4	3.3	10.6	16.3	19.2	17.8	13.1	7.2	0.2	-8.6	4.4
		mm	86	77	69	75	81	102	108	103	106	82	100	101	1090
Schefferville (Que.)	512	°C	-22.7	-21.2	-14.8	-6.9	0.9	8.5	12.6	10.8	5.6	-0.9	-8.7	-18.1	-4.6
		mm	41	37	37	35	45	79	89	98	83	70	64	46	724
Val d'Or (Que.)	338	°C	-16.7	-14.4	-8.3	1.3	8.4	14.6	17.1	15.4	10.8	4.9	-2.9	-12.7	1.5
		mm	57	55	55	46	58	90	90	101	105	78	91	69	901
Fredericton (N.B.)	40	°C	-9.2	-8.5	-2.6	4.0	10.5	15.7	19.1	18.0	13.6	7.9	1.8	-6.3	5.3
		mm	91	86	73	81	88	86	90	86	87	91	120	105	1084
Moncton (N.B.)	76	°C	-8.1	-7.7	-2.8	3.6	9.8	14.9	18.6	17.5	13.2	7.8	2.3	-5.3	5.3
		mm	107	100	93	84	80	91	80	80	73	91	112	108	1099
Saint John (N.B.)	36	°C	-6.5	-5.7	-1.2	4.3	9.5	13.6	16.7	16.3	13.8	9.1	3.7	-3.3	5.9
		mm	126	114	98	100	103	94	90	100	100	105	145	132	1307
Sydney (N.S.)	60	°C	-4.4	-5.5	-2.4	2.2	7.7	13.0	17.9	17.8	13.9	8.9	4.2	-1.5	6.0
		mm	137	119	119	95	100	81	78	100	99	112	161	140	1341
Yarmouth (N.S.)	41	°C	-2.7	-2.9	0.2	4.6	9.3	13.3	16.4	16.4	13.9	9.8	5.4	-0.2	7.0
		mm	141	116	102	99	101	87	74	96	86	108	139	134	1283
Charlottetown (P.E.I.)	57	°C	-6.7	-7.2	-3.2	2.3	8.6	14.1	18.4	17.9	13.9	8.6	3.3	-3.6	5.6
		mm	98	82	76	75	80	79	74	90	92	99	115	110	1060
Gander (Nfld.)	147	°C	-6.1	-6.3	-3.6	0.8	6.3	11.4	16.5	15.8	11.8	6.3	1.9	-3.4	4.3
		mm	94	101	97	85	62	76	78	101	84	95	107	98	1078
St. John's (Nfld.)	141	°C	-3.8	-4.2	-2.4	1.1	5.5	10.4	15.3	15.4	11.9	7.1	3.5	-1.3	4.9
		mm	145	156	133	114	99	89	83	113	112	139	161	167	1511
Dawson (Y.T.)	324	°C	-28.6	-23.0	-14.1	-1.8	7.8	13.9	15.5	12.7	6.4	-3.2	-16.5	-25.3	-4.7
		mm	19	16	13	9	22	37	53	51	28	27	25	26	326
Iqaluit (Frobisher Bay) (N.W.T.)	207	°C	-26.2	-25.2	-22.3	-14.2	-3.3	3.5	7.9	6.9	2.4	-4.7	-12.4	-20.3	-9.0
		mm	24	28	21	22	23	38	53	58	43	42	37	26	415
Yellowknife (N.W.T.)	208	°C	-28.6	-25.7	-18.6	-7.8	4.0	12.2	16.0	14.1	6.8	-1.2	-14.2	-23.8	-5.6
		mm	14	12	12	10	14	17	33	36	28	31	24	18	249

- Name three places that have maximum temperatures in August.

  (One place is the same as in July.) _____

  _____

- What is the highest monthly mean temperature in the place closest

  to you? _____ °C

- What is the range of temperature in the place nearest to

  you? _____ °C

5. (a) Complete climographs (an example is given on page 54 of the textbook) for the places that your teacher tells you. Fill in the names of those places you are to plot below.

_____ _____ _____

_____ _____ _____

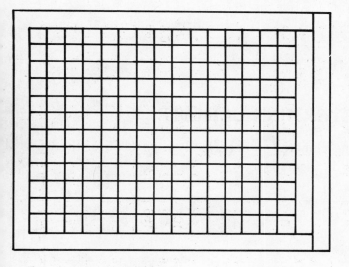
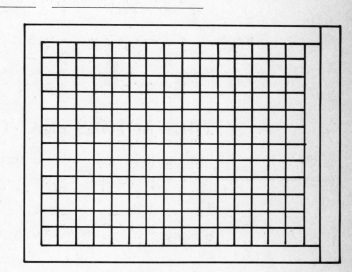

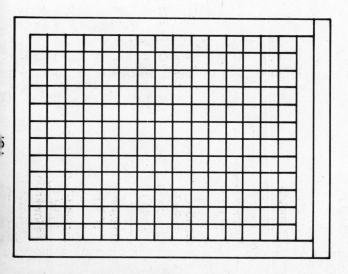
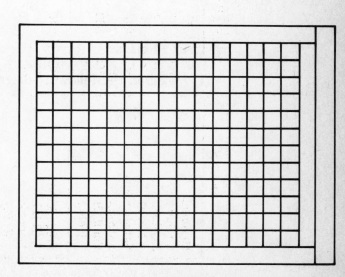

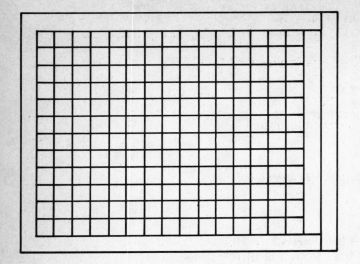
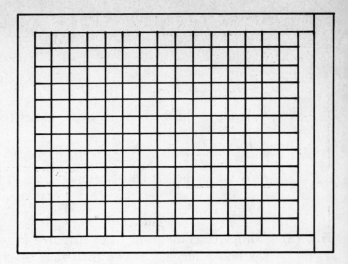

(b) In your own notebook, compare and contrast (describe the differences and similarities between) the temperature and precipitation at the places indicated by your teacher. Fill in the names of those places here.

_____

_____

THE FACTORS THAT DETERMINE CLIMATE

p. 55

List the four factors that determine climate, as described on page 55 of the textbook.

1. _____

2. _____

3. _____

4. _____

LATITUDE

1.   Fill in the following diagram using Figure 2-44 on page 56 of the textbook.

The rays are more

_____ _____ , and

do not have

much _____

_____ .

ATMOSPHERE

The rays pass through more

_____ , so they are _____

when they reach the _____ .

SUN'S RAY

80°N

SUN'S RAY

70°N

The rays are

more _____

and are therefore

_____ .

60°N

CANADA

U.S.A.

50°N

40°N

The rays pass through less

_____ , so they

are _____

when they reach

the _____ .

2. (a) Using page 55 of your textbook and the climate figures found on pages
         61 and 62 of this workbook, fill in the following details. You will need to
         use the index in your atlas to get latitudes.

LOCATION	AVERAGE YEARLY TEMPERATURE °C	LATITUDE °N
Resolute	_____	_____
Iqaluit (Frobisher Bay)	_____	_____
Schefferville	_____	_____
Goose Bay	_____	_____
Toronto	_____	_____

    (b) Fill in the blanks.

         As latitude increases (gets higher), temperature _____ .

         As latitude decreases, temperatures _____ .

You can see, by examining temperatures from all over Canada, that latitude does *not* always determine temperature. Other factors may even cause temperatures to increase in higher latitudes.

WIND DIRECTION AND THE PRESENCE OF WATER BODIES

p. 57

1. Copy the words from the three diagrams on page 57 of the textbook onto the diagrams below. After referring to the written description on page 57, fill in the blanks beside each diagram.

Bodies of water, especially _____,

provide most of the _____ needed

to create _____. The winds carry

this _____ onto the _____,

where it may fall as _____ or _____.

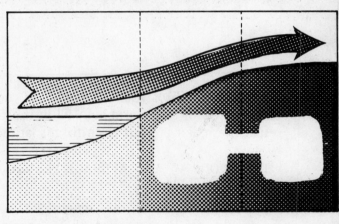

In early summer, winds blowing

over the cooler water keep the coastal

areas _____.

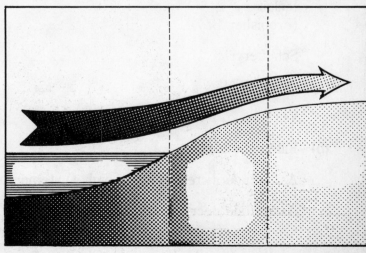

In early winter, the waters are

somewhat _____
  (warmer/colder)
than the land, and winds blowing over

this water keep the coastal areas

_____.

2. When you circled the dates of minimum and maximum temperatures (pages 61 and 62 in the workbook), you found that these occurred normally in January and July respectively. A few places, especially those along the east coast, were different.

(a) Why do many coastal areas have their lowest temperatures in February rather than in January? (Look at the diagrams which you have just drawn.)

_____

_____

_____

(b) Why do some coastal areas have their highest temperatures in August rather than in July?

_____

_____

_____

MOUNTAIN RANGES AND ALTITUDE

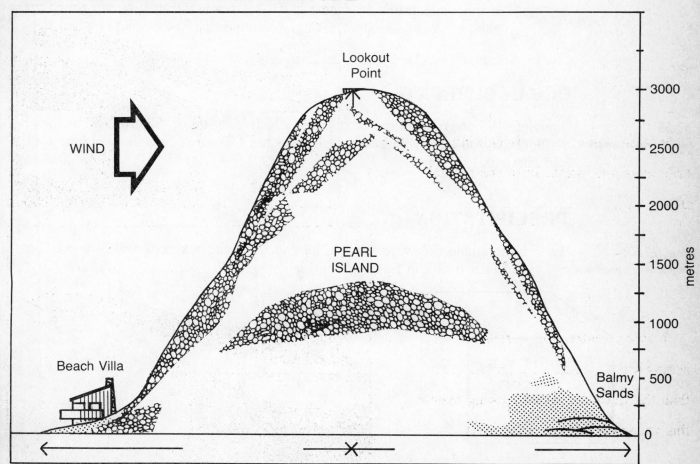

1. Temperatures drop by _____ °C for every 100 m increase in _____ (height above sea level). Mountains also have an effect on _____ . More precipitation falls on the _____ side than on the _____ side of a mountain.

2. Using Figure 2-49 on page 58 of the textbook as a guide, mark on the diagram of Pearl Island

    (a) windward and leeward in the correct positions
    (b) where clouds and rain are most likely to occur.

3. (a) If you were on vacation and hoped to get a suntan, would you

    stay at Beach Villa or at Balmy Sands? _____

    Why? _____

    _____

    (b) If the temperature at the sea level is 30°C, what is the temperature at Lookout Point (assuming that temperatures decrease by 0.6°C for

    every 100 m increase in altitude)? _____ °C

    (c) If the temperature in winter is 6°C at sea level, how far up would you have to go to see snow falling? (Assume that snow will fall when the

    temperature is 0°C.) _____ m

OCEAN CURRENTS

Complete the diagram on the next page, which is based on Figure 2-50 in the textbook. If you have coloured pencils, use red for warm currents and blue for cold currents.

PRECIPITATION

1. Unscramble the words (pages 59 and 60 of the textbook will help you). WATER exists in three states:

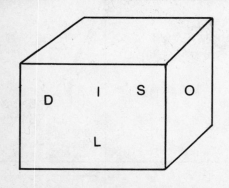

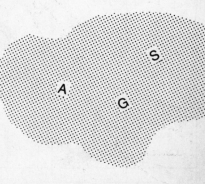

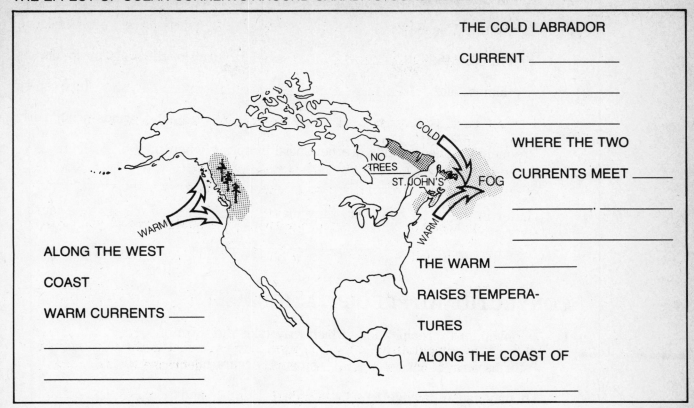

THE COLD LABRADOR

CURRENT _____

_____

_____

WHERE THE TWO

CURRENTS MEET _____

_____ . _____

_____

THE WARM _____

RAISES TEMPERA-

TURES

ALONG THE COAST OF

_____

ALONG THE WEST

COAST

WARM CURRENTS _____

_____

_____

2. When the water in puddles _____, it is changed to an
                                      (SEROVAEPAT)
    invisible gas in the air, which is called _____ .When this
                                                  (ATERW) (OPVAUR)
    vapour is cooled, it _____ to form tiny droplets. When
                              (NOCNDESSE)
    these tiny droplets mass together, they form _____ .
                                                        (OLCUDS)

OROGRAPHIC PRECIPITATION

1. Complete the diagram from page 61 in the textbook.   *pp. 60-61*

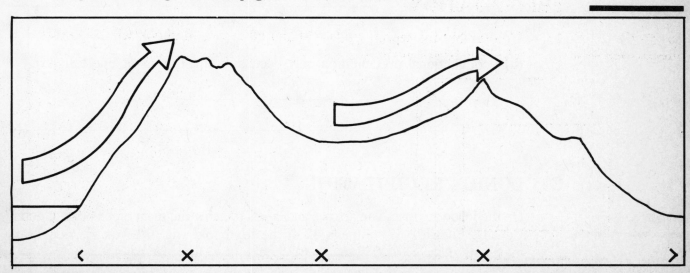

2/Canada's Physical Base **69**

2. Fill in the blanks.

In western Canada the _____ slopes are wetter because
                        (western/eastern)
they are on the _____ side. In many of the valleys, conditions
                (leeward/windward)
are almost like _____ . In western

_____, _____ winds occur fairly
        (province)
frequently. These winds are beneficial in spring when they _____

_____ .

Later in the year, however, they may _____ causing

_____ .

CONVECTIONAL PRECIPITATION

p. 61

1. Convectional precipitation, which may take the form of _____

storms and _____ storms, occurs mainly in the _____ .
                                                          (season)
It may cause damage to _____ and _____ .

2. Explain what causes convectional precipitation.

_____

_____

3. Complete the diagram at the top of page 62 in the textbook.——————→

4. Why do you think that

   (a) conventional precipitation is more common in the Prairie Provinces
       than in other parts of Canada?

   _____

   _____

   (b) convectional precipitation only occurs in small areas at one time?

   _____

   _____

CYCLONIC PRECIPITATION

p. 62

1. On the following map, use arrows and labels to show the main types of air affecting
   Canada. Figure 2-57, on page 62 of the textbook, will give you the necessary
   information. ———————————————————————→

CONVECTIONAL PRECIPITATION AND ITS EFFECTS IN THE PRAIRIE PROVINCES

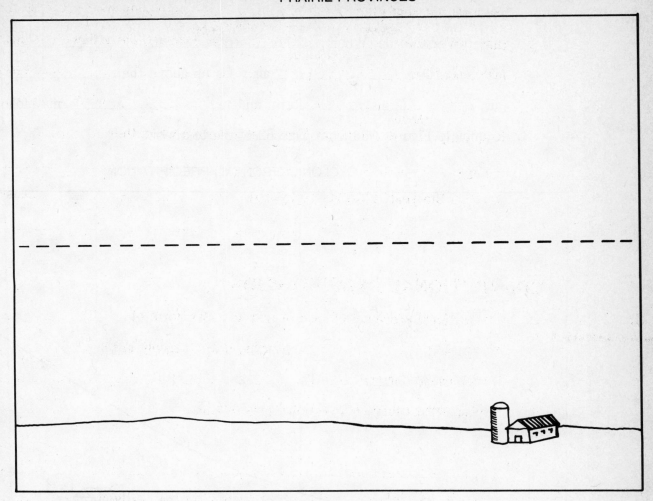

MAIN TYPES OF AIR AFFECTING CANADA

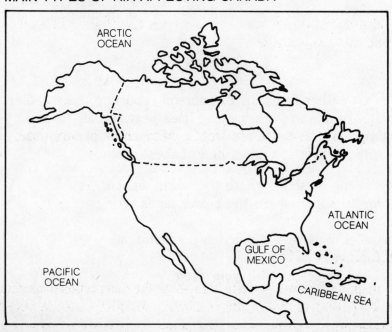

2. Fill in the blanks, using page 62 of the textbook to help.

Several different _____ _____

meet over Canada. When _____ and _____

air meet, the _____ air rises up above the _____

air, _____ form, and _____ may follow.

3. Complete Figure 2-58 from page 62 of the textbook.

CYCLONIC (FRONTAL) PRECIPITATION

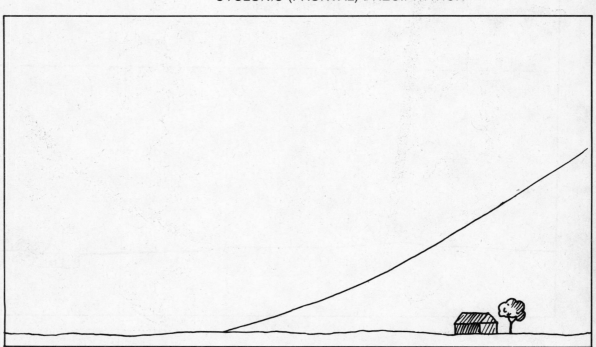

WEATHER MAPS

Research

When you see or hear a weather forecast, the person reporting the weather often refers to "fronts." Fronts are the dividing lines between air masses; precipitation usually occurs where there are fronts. Many newspapers print weather maps showing these fronts. Collect one of these maps.

1. Use a light red shading to show where the warm air is.
2. Use a blue shading to show where the colder air is.
3. Label the fronts.
4. Shade in with parallel lines where there is precipitation.
5. Mark in where you live.
6. Write down what the forecast is for your area.

DISTRIBUTION OF PRECIPITATION IN CANADA

1. On this map of Canada, the country has been divided up into three regions. Complete the diagram by filling in details that can be found following Figure 2-56 on page 62 of the textbook.

pp. 62-63

MAJOR TYPES OF PRECIPITATION IN CANADA

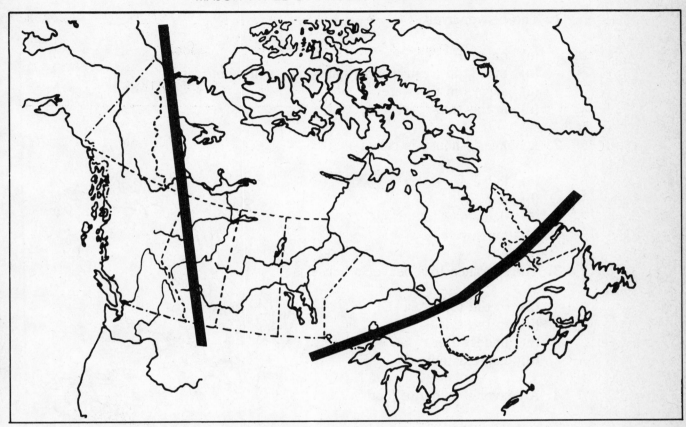

2. Much to the surprise of many people the Canadian Arctic is a huge desert.

    (a) Why is it called a desert? _____

    _____

    (b) List four reasons why it is so dry.

    (i) _____

    (ii) _____

    (iii) _____

    (iv) _____

VEGETATION, SOILS, AND ANIMALS

Research

Pick the right information to complete these sentences about the beaver. You may need to look it up in nature books or encyclopedias, or get the information from your parents, teacher, or friends.

1. The beaver lives

   (a) on land
   (b) mostly in fresh water, sometimes going onto land
   (c) always in the water
   (d) in the sea.

2. A beaver's house is called a

   (a) lodge
   (b) den
   (c) dam
   (d) burrow.

3. The entrance to a beaver's house is

   (a) in the top
   (b) in the side
   (c) underwater
   (d) non-existent.

4. A beaver's favourite food is

   (a) spruce tree needles
   (b) grass
   (c) waterweed
   (d) the bark of poplar trees.

5. Beavers build dams to

   (a) keep the level of the water up
   (b) trap fish
   (c) store their food
   (d) prevent their enemies from reaching them.

6. Explain, in as much detail as you can, how the beaver's life would be affected by changes in climate. Remember the indirect effect that climate and weather will have on vegetation and water levels. Use your own paper and write in proper sentence form.

VEGETATION

1. **(a)** Natural vegetation is _____ *p. 64*

_____ .

(b) Why is there very little natural vegetation left in southern Canada?

_____

_____

_____

2. Copy details from page 65 of your textbook onto the map below. Use four colours on your map and include these colours in the correct places on the key. Write in the words on the map, too.

NATURAL VEGETATION REGIONS OF CANADA

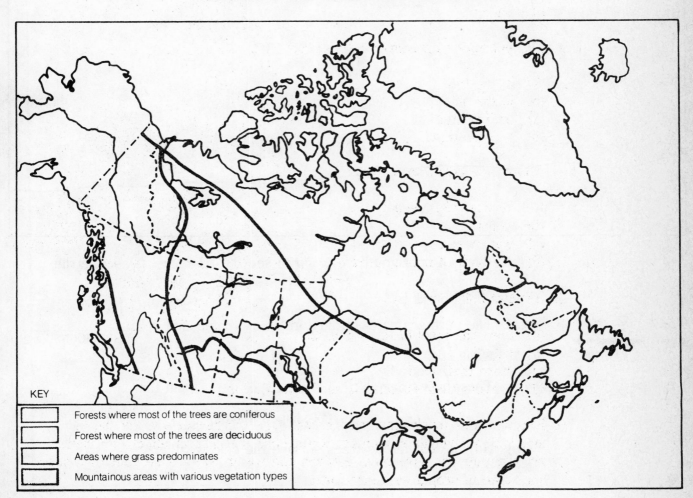

KEY

☐ Forests where most of the trees are coniferous

☐ Forest where most of the trees are deciduous

☐ Areas where grass predominates

☐ Mountainous areas with various vegetation types

3. Tundra vegetation grows in the _____ where winters are _____ and _____ . Tundra plants grow very _____ , _____ , and _____ during the short summer season. The most common types of tundra plants are _____ and _____ . In the southern parts of the Arctic, where it is warmer, _____ plants grow and they also grow much _____ .

4. **(a)** Draw and fully label a diagram to show what is meant by the tree line.

THE TREE LINE

(b) Where would you have to go to see the tree line? (Describe the nearest place to your home.) _____

p. 67

5. **(a)** The northern parts of our forests are composed of _____ (REFIOCNSUO) trees such as _____ or _____ . These trees have _____ and thin _____ -shaped leaves.

(b) How do coniferous trees survive the cold weather?

_____

_____

_____

6. **(a)** In the southern parts of our forests there are more _____
(DCIUSUOED)

trees such as _____ and _____ .

A deciduous tree has _____ flat leaves,

which it _____ in autumn.

(b) What does a deciduous tree do with its sap to survive the winter?

_____

_____

(c) Why would shedding its leaves be important for it to survive, too?

_____

_____

7. The largest trees in Canada are the _____ . They

grow along the _____ coast because the climate is

very _____ .

8. **(a)** Why can grass survive in the southern Prairies when trees cannot?

p. 68

_____

_____

_____

_____

_____

(b) Look at Figure 2-68 in your textbook. How long may the roots of one healthy grass plant be (adding all of the roots together, of course)?

_____

(c) Name a city or town that is that distance away from you. Refer to

your atlas for help. _____

9. **(a)** Complete the diagram in Figure 2-69 (a) from page 68 in your
textbook. ⟶

(b) Why do vegetation types change as you go up a mountain? _____

_____

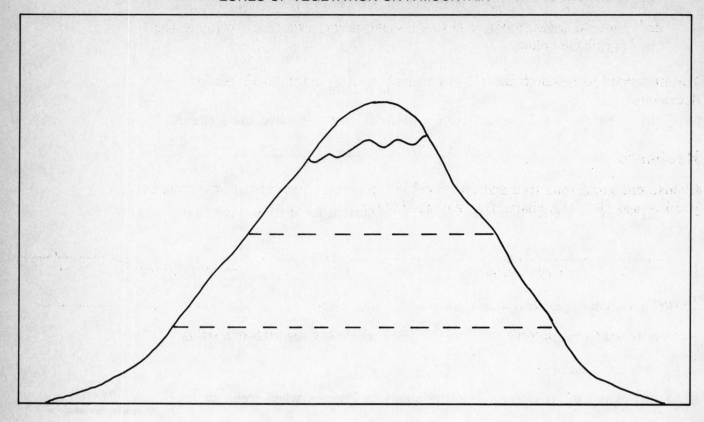

Tree Study

1. **(a)** Circle the names of the trees in this puzzle.
Put a check mark in the left-hand column next
to the ones on the list as you find them.

C or D

W	M	O	R	A	D	E	C
H	A	W	T	H	O	R	N
K	P	L	R	E	L	M	S
W	L	O	N	R	A	E	P
F	E	I	P	U	U	N	R
I	P	Y	T	L	T	K	U
R	M	A	S	L	A	B	C
W	O	L	L	I	W	R	E

BALSAM
CEDAR
ELM
FIR
HAWTHORN
MAPLE
OAK
PEAR
PINE
POPLAR
SPRUCE
WALNUT
WILLOW
YEW

When you have finished, the letters that are left will spell a word that
is found on all trees.

(b) The word is _____ .

(c) Write C (coniferous) or D (deciduous) beside each tree's name in the right-hand column.

You may need to research these trees to find out if they are coniferous or deciduous.

Research

Choose one coniferous tree and one deciduous tree that grow in the area where you live and fill in this chart. You may need library books to help.

CONIFEROUS TREE	DECIDUOUS TREE
NAME _____	NAME _____
Shape viewed from a distance	Shape viewed from a distance
LEAF AND CONE	LEAF (plus flower, catkin, seed and/or fruit if possible).

MAIN USES OR IMPORTANCE

MAIN USES OR IMPORTANCE

SOIL

pp. 69-70

1. Fill in the following chart to describe what soil is composed of.

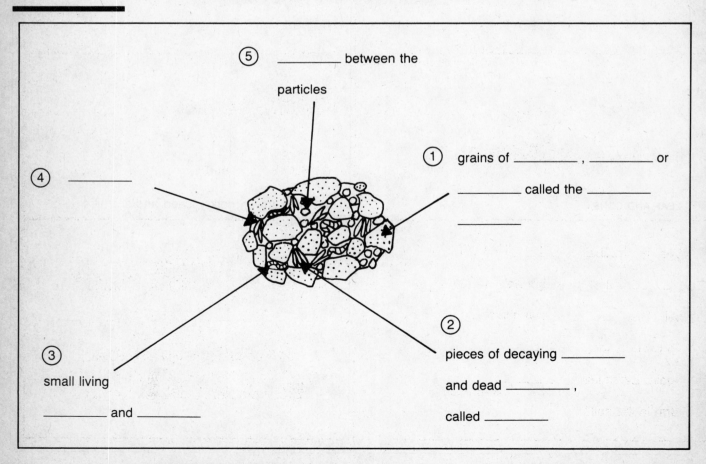

⑤ _____ between the

particles

④ _____

① grains of _____ , _____ or

_____ called the _____

_____

② pieces of decaying _____

and dead _____ ,

called _____

③ small living

_____ and _____

2. How long does it take for a soil to form? _____

_____

3. Fill in the blanks in the following diagram.

p. 70

HOW A SOIL IS FORMED

The _____ are broken down into

_____ _____ by _____

and _____ . The pieces either

stay _____ _____ or are washed into

a _____ , where they _____ _____ .

_____ start to grow on the loose

rock _____ . Their _____ help to

break up the _____ more. _____

roots and leaves collect _____

and _____ the _____ soil.

Small _____, especially _____ ,

mix the _____ matter in

with the _____ matter.

The rain washes _____

_____ down through the

soil. The _____ draws them

up towards the _____

again. Eventually, _____

form in the soil.

4. The different layers of a soil make up the _____

_____ . Most of Canada has _____

soils, which have a _____ a few centimetres below the

surface.

    The richest soils in Canada are found in the _____

of the _____ . These soils are _____ ,

_____ , and _____ , and the best

ones are called _____ _____ .

p. 71   **5.** Copy Figure 2-72 from page 71 of your textbook.

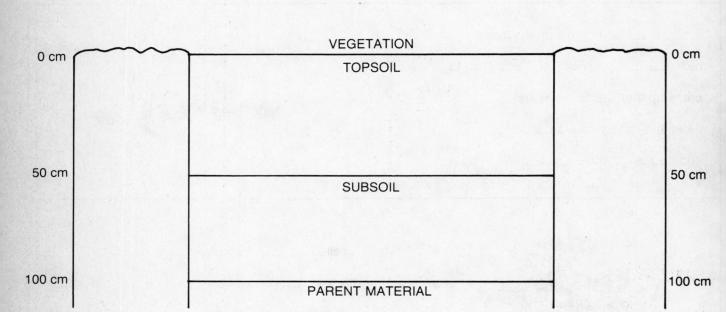

6. Insert one of the following words in the gap wherever it is suitable (one
word fits in each gap): dark, vary, fertile, Prairies, plants, downward,
humus

    Soils in Canada are best in the southern _____ where

it is fairly dry. The dead grass forms _____ in the soil.

This gives it a _____ colour and helps to keep it

_____ .

    In most other parts of Canada, soils are poorer because the rain, trickling through the soil, washes nutrients _____ . In

the Arctic areas the soils are thin and stony. They are not very fertile

because the _____ do not supply enough humus. Along

the west coast and mountains, soils _____ greatly from

place to place.

If you can find a place where soil layers show (in a road cut or the side of a
valley), draw and describe them as accurately as you can.
Use page 71 of the textbook as a guide.

LOCATION: _____   *SOIL PROFILE*

```
0 cm ┌──────────────────┐
10  ┤                  │
20  ┤                  │
30  ┤                  │
40  ┤                  │
50  ┤                  │
60  ┤                  │
70  ┤                  │
80  ┤                  │
90  ┤                  │
100 ┤                  │
    └                  │
```

ANIMALS

1. **(a)** What is meant by

    species? _____

    extinct? _____

    (b) Why are some species of animals in danger of becoming extinct?

    _____

    _____

p. 72

2. For a period of one week keep a list of wild animals (including birds, fish, and insects) that you see around your home or school. Fill in this table.

TYPE OF ANIMAL	WHERE IT LIVES	WHAT IT EATS	WHAT IT WOULD EAT IN ITS NATURAL ENVIRONMENT

PATTERNS OF WILDLIFE

1. **(a)** What is meant by habitat? _____ *p. 73*

(b) How would you describe your habitat? _____

_____

2. Look at the four maps on page 73 of your textbook showing where some animals live, and fill in the details. (You may need to get information from your library.)

(a)

The moose lives mainly in areas where there are plenty of _____ growing. The reason why it needs this habitat is that _____

_____ .

(b)

The pronghorn antelope seems to thrive in areas where the natural vegetation is _____ . This is because it _____

_____ .

(c)

The polar bear is restricted to areas that are in _____ Canada, very close to the _____ or on_____ . This is because they eat _____ . They usually only come onto land when it is time to _____ .

(d)

Ermine live in just about all parts of Canada except in the _____ . This means that they are very adaptable to different environments. Their food includes _____

_____ .

p. 74

3. **(a)** Why do some animals migrate? _____

_____

Give two examples of animals that migrate. _____ _____

(b) Why do some animals hibernate? _____

_____

Give two examples of animals that hibernate. _____ _____

The Flyway Game

Play this game with one or two other people. See which of you manages to reach the finish first.

You will need dice. The person who rolls the highest number starts. The first person to reach or pass the finish wins. (If you do not have dice, write the numbers 1 to 6 on a six-sided pencil, and roll it to find numbers.)

Use small markers or pieces of paper to move along the flyway route.

Briefly describe what happened to you along the flyway route. _____

_____

_____

_____

_____

_____

EXTINCTION OF ANIMALS

p. 76

Read the account on page 76 of the textbook.

1. **(a)** What is meant by endangered species? _____

_____

(b) How many endangered species of animals are there in Canada? _____
There are also many plants that are endangered.

Research

p. 77

2. Choose any of the endangered animals illustrated on page 77 (or choose an animal native to your part of the country and acceptable to your teacher). Answer these questions. You will need to use your library.

(a) The animal I am studying is the _____.

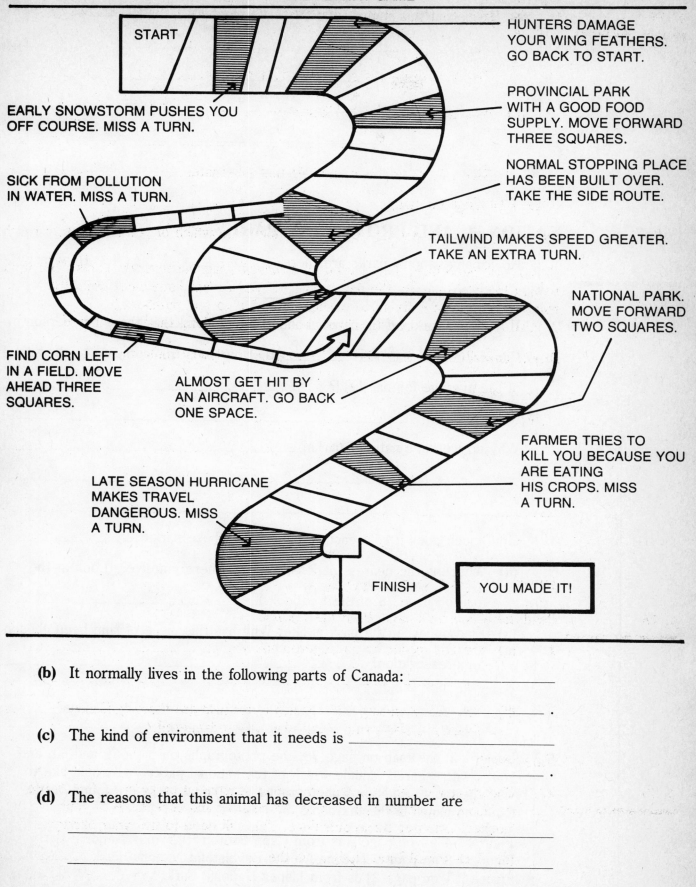

(b) It normally lives in the following parts of Canada: _____

_____ .

(c) The kind of environment that it needs is _____

_____ .

(d) The reasons that this animal has decreased in number are

_____

_____

_____ .

(e) To permit this animal to increase its numbers I suggest that

_____

_____

_____

_____

_____ .

NATIONAL AND PROVINCIAL PARKS

p. 78

1. How many national parks are there? _____ How many

    provincial parks? _____

2. How much parkland (in national and provincial parks) is there per person in

    Canada? _____ ha. How does this compare to the size

    of the average football field? _____

    _____

3. Why do we have national parks? _____

    _____

    _____

4. How much does it cost each of us to keep these parks? _____

5. **(a)** Where is the nearest national park to where you live? (Look at the

    map on page 78 of the textbook.) _____

    (b) Find out what the park is like. Why has this piece of land been chosen

    for preservation? _____

    _____

    _____

6. Looking at the map on page 78, the photographs on page 79 and 80, and
    your own research, decide which of the national parks you would like to
    visit the most. Additional photographs of national parks are found on the
    following pages in the textbook:

    Figure 1-4 (c) on page 4 is from Cape Breton Highlands National Park.
    Figure 1-8 on page 7 is from Mount Revelstoke National Park.
    Figure 2-1 on page 31 is from Jasper National Park.
    Figure 2-16 on page 37 is from Glacier National Park.

Figure 2-17 on page 37 is from Jasper National Park.
Figure 6-3 on page 183 (skiing) is from Terra Nova National Park.
Figure 6-3 on page 183 (gulls) is from St. Lawrence Islands National Park.

I would like to visit _____ National Park. This is

because _____

_____

_____

_____ .

TERRA NOVA NATIONAL PARK

1. Read the description of Terra Nova National Park on page 80 of the
    textbook. The map of the park (from page 81) is reproduced sideways on
    the next page.

p. 80

2. Answer question 61(b) from the textbook using this map. Use colours to
    distinguish water, rivers, roads, and so on. Include a key, scale, and north
    sign.

FACILITY THAT I HAVE INCLUDED	THE KIND OF PEOPLE WHO WOULD USE IT

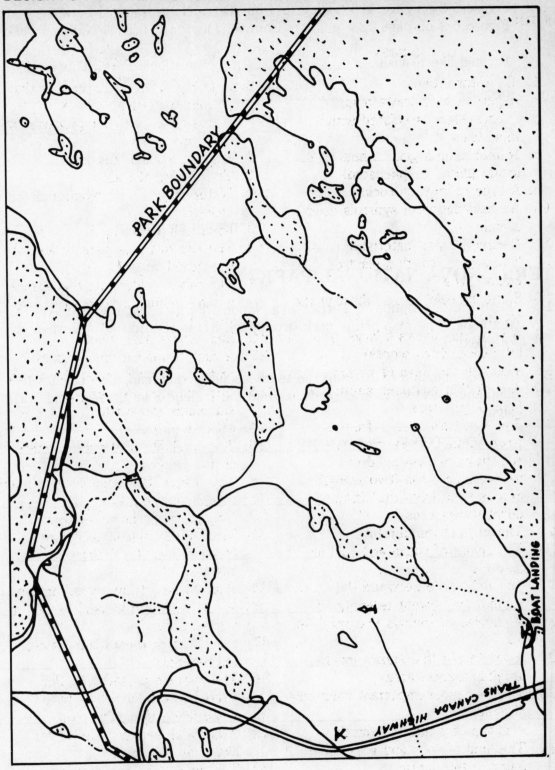

3.   Answer question 61(c) on page 81 of the textbook. Fill in the table about your design for the park.

VOCABULARY CROSSWORD

Clues

ACROSS

1. To water crops
3. A person who draws maps
5. Precipitation associated with mountains
6. Numbers on a grid to help you locate places (hyphenated)
8. A type of igneous rock
10. An explanation of symbols used on a map
11. Decaying plant material in a soil
14. The area in which a plant or animal lives
15. Some animals _____ through the winter.
16. A map that shows a large area but little detail (two words)
18. Water in the form of a gas
20. A rock that has been altered by heat or pressure
21. Some animals _____ from one place to another every year.
24. A pattern of lines used on topographic maps (two words)
27. Soil as seen from the surface down (two words)
29. The highest temperature
31. The result of warm and cold air meeting
33. The difference between the highest and lowest temperature
34. A species of animals that may die out
35. A map scale that shows much detail in a small area
36. The four most important compass directions
41. A group of plants or animals
45. The kind of soils and vegetation found in the Arctic
46. A statement of the scale of a map
48. Height above sea level
49. A shape or pattern on a map that represents an object
52. A way of representing scale, using numbers only

DOWN

2. A group of plants or animals that no longer exists
3. A line on a map joining places with the same height
4. A poor, leached soil
7. The rotting of rock
9. Water may _____ when it is heated.
12. Rock in liquid form
13. The remains of a plant or animal preserved in rock
17. The mixture of plants that grows without human interference (two words)
19. Rain, snow, hail, sleet
22. A rock formed from layers of particles, usually under the ocean
23. The mixture of gases that surrounds the earth
25. Masses of ice
26. The condition of the atmosphere at any moment
28. The height difference between one contour and the next
30. Change from vapour to liquid
31. The kind of rainfall occurring frequently in the Prairies in summer
32. Rock formed from cooling magma
35. A _____ graph is used to plot temperature.
37. _____ mum means the lowest temperature.
38. The average condition of the atmosphere over a long time
39. Deep inlets along the coast
40. A detailed map that shows the shape of the land
42. The amount of reduction used when drawing a map
43. A zone north of which trees do not grow very well (two words)
44. The wearing down of the land surface

53. A way of showing monthly precipitation and temperatures throughout the year
54. A tree that has cones
55. The part of a soil that starts as rock is called the _____ matter.
56. A rich, fertile soil of the southern Prairies
57. A maple is a _____ tree.
58. A striped metamorphic rock

47. A sedimentary rock made of sand particles
50. To move a map so that north is in the correct direction
51. Another word for legend

The answers are in the vocabulary on page 82 of the textbook and in Chapter 2.

PERSONAL PROGRESS CHART

Put a check mark in the first square for each section when your teacher assigns it. When you have completed the section, put a check mark in the second square.

Page	Topic	Assigned by teacher	Completed by you
94	The First Canadians _____	☐	☐
95	An Arctic Adventure _____	☐	☐
95	The Inuit People _____	☐	☐
97	The Resolute Experiment _____	☐	☐
98	The Indian People _____	☐	☐
104	More Recent Immigrants _____	☐	☐
106	A Case Study: Michael Pryszlak _____	☐	☐
109	Immigration to Canada _____	☐	☐
111	Vocabulary Crossword _____	☐	☐

THE FIRST CANADIANS

p. 85

1.   Less than _____ years ago the area we know as

Canada lay quiet and almost empty. The human population consisted only

of _____ native people. Essentially, the Indians

occupied the land _____ , while

the Inuit lived _____ .

2. The word Inuit means _____ .

Eskimo, which means _____ , is a term the Inuit

prefer not to use.

3. There is one theory that tries to explain how the native people arrived in

North America. About _____ years ago there was an

Ice Age. At that time a _____ joined _____

and North America. Many Indians and Inuit wandered across this land

bridge, probably _____ .

AN ARCTIC ADVENTURE

Read the "Arctic Adventure" on page 87 in your textbook, and then list below
the five steps you would take in order to survive.

p. 87

1. _____

_____

2. _____

_____

3. _____

_____

4. _____

_____

5. _____

_____

THE INUIT PEOPLE

1. In your own words describe how the Inuit made use of all parts of their
environment. Use correct sentences.

p. 87

_____

_____

_____

_____

p. 88

2. How has traditional Inuit life changed as a result of contact with white people from the south?

p. 89

3. There are six problems that develop when one culture meets another culture. Describe them.

(a)

(b)

(c)

(d) _____

_____

(e) _____

_____

(f) _____

_____

THE RESOLUTE EXPERIMENT

1. Answer question 5 on page 89 of your textbook using this base map of Canada.

Mark the place where you live on the map. Write in its name, too.

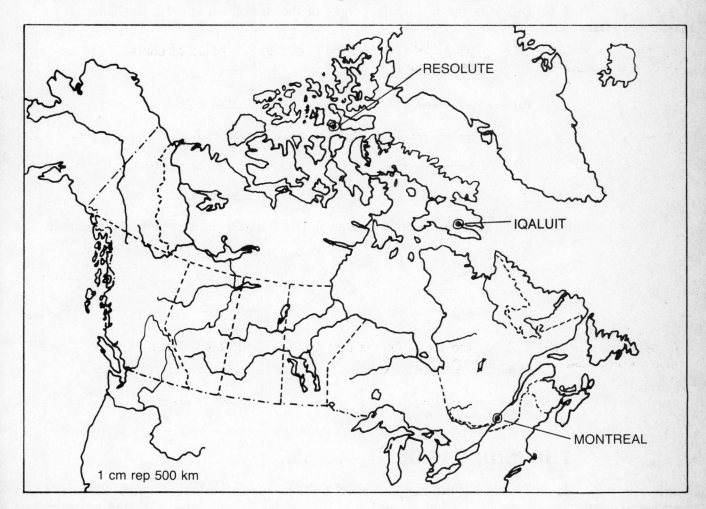

1 cm rep 500 km

(a) If I lived in Resolute, the nearest town would be as far away

as _____ is from where I live now.

(b) If I lived in Resolute, the nearest city would be as far away

as _____ is from where I live now.

p. 91 **2.** Using the same base map of Canada as in question 1, answer question 6 on page 91 of your textbook.

_____

_____

_____

p. 90 **3.** Why was the decision made to build a new town in Resolute? Give two reasons.

(a) _____

(b) _____

p. 93 **4.** Describe the three advantages of the new town site for Resolute.

(a) _____

_____

(b) _____

_____

(c) _____

_____

5. What advantages and/or disadvantages would the new town of Resolute have for the Inuit in particular?

_____

_____

_____

_____

_____

THE INDIAN PEOPLE

p. 95 **1.** On the accompanying map of Canada, mark the various areas that were occupied by Indian and Inuit groups. Be sure to label each Indian group as well as the Inuit group.

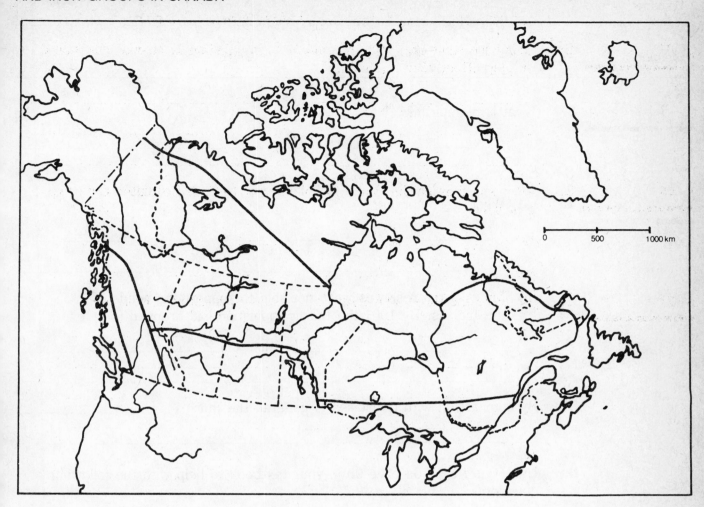

2. Read pages 96 to 97 in the textbook, and then fill in the following chart.   *pp. 96-97*

THE PLAINS INDIANS

FEATURE OF THEIR WAY OF LIFE	DESCRIPTION OF EACH FEATURE
Environment and climate	
Source of food	
Methods of killing animals	
Housing	

Transportation	
Clothing	

p. 96

3. What is pemmican?

_____

_____

p. 97

4. **(a)** What are reserves?

_____

_____

(b) Many of the reserves were not able to support the needs of the Indians. By 1901 the Indian population had dropped to

_____ because of _____

_____ .

5. By comparison with Canadians in general, the Indians _____

_____ .

6. Use Figure 3-17 on page 98 in your textbook to help with the following question.

Imagine that you were a teenager growing up on a reserve. Write a one page letter, using the correct letter-writing method, to a non-Indian in a Canadian city. Your letter should explain why many of your friends and relatives had to struggle to solve their problems. You should give names to these imaginary people and include at least three of the reasons given in Figure 3-17. Make it a personal letter. Write the letter in your notebook.

7. **(a)** Draw bar graphs which show the improvements which have been made in supplying piped water to people on Indian reserves in each region of Canada. The first region is plotted for you.

(b) Use three colours, one for 1977 columns, one for 1984, and the other for improvements (1977-1984).

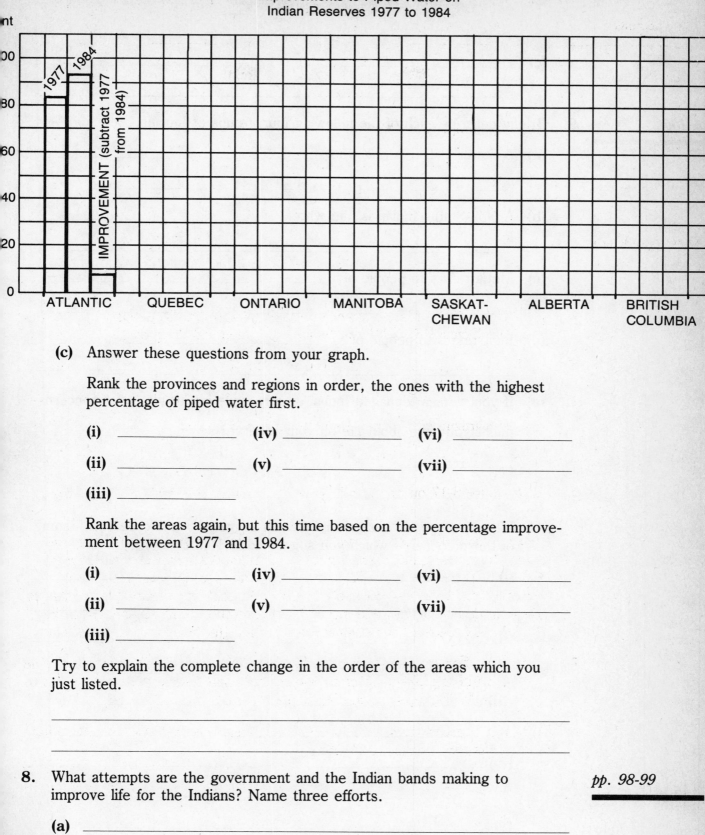

Improvements to Piped Water on Indian Reserves 1977 to 1984

(c) Answer these questions from your graph.

Rank the provinces and regions in order, the ones with the highest percentage of piped water first.

(i) _____ **(iv)** _____ **(vi)** _____

(ii) _____ **(v)** _____ **(vii)** _____

(iii) _____

Rank the areas again, but this time based on the percentage improvement between 1977 and 1984.

(i) _____ **(iv)** _____ **(vi)** _____

(ii) _____ **(v)** _____ **(vii)** _____

(iii) _____

Try to explain the complete change in the order of the areas which you just listed.

_____

_____

8. What attempts are the government and the Indian bands making to improve life for the Indians? Name three efforts.

pp. 98-99

(a) _____

_____

(b) _____

(c) _____

p. 100

9. Briefly describe each of the following four groups of Indians.

(a) A Status Indian is one who _____ .

(b) A Non-Status Indian is one who _____ .

(c) Metis refers to people of _____ .

(d) Inuit refers to people of _____ .

10. **(a)** If you were a teenaged Indian on a reserve in Canada, what concerns might you have about life on your reserve? _____

(b) What five specific changes might you suggest to try to deal with some of those concerns which you suggested in 10(a)?

(i) _____

(ii) _____

(iii) _____

(iv) _____

(v) _____

11. Using the following chart, compare the traditional Inuit and the Plains Indians. Base your answers on pages 85 to 100 in the textbook.

BASIS OF COMPARISON	TRADITIONAL INUIT	PLAINS INDIANS
What their natural environment is like		
Five specific items in their environment and how they used them to survive		
Some changes they have experienced from their traditional way of life		
Current difficulties they face		
Signs of progress for the future		

MORE RECENT IMMIGRANTS

p. 100

1. **(a)** What does emigrate mean? _____

_____

(b) Give the meaning of immigrant. _____

_____

(c) Fill in the blanks below with either immigrant or emigrant.

- An English man leaves his home country to come to live in Canada.

In England he is considered an _____ .

In Canada he is considered an _____ .

- A woman leaves her home in Nigeria to come to live in Canada.

In Nigeria she is thought of as an _____ .

In Canada she is an _____ .

- A Canadian student moves to the United States to live.

For Canada that student is an _____ .

For the United States that student is an _____ .

2. **(a)** A pull factor means _____

_____

Three examples of pull factors are _____ ,

_____ , and _____ .

(b) A push factor means _____

_____

Three examples of push factors are _____ ,

_____ , and _____ .

3. Canada has a multicultural society, which means it has a _____

_____

_____

p. 101

4. Answer question 18 using the outline for the family tree below. Use the family tree on page 102 in the textbook to help.

Great-grandparents └────────┴───────┴────────┴─────────┴───────┴───────┘

Grandparents └──────────┴──────────┘   └──────────┴──────────┘

Parents └────────────────────────────┴──────────────────────────┘

Your mother   Your father
born . . .   born . . .

Sisters and ┌──┐
brothers   Your name is

_____

Include any brothers or sisters beside your name.

5. Answer questions 23 (a) and (b) on page 104 of the textbook.

(a) Cultural baggage means _____ *p. 104*

_____ .

(b) The cultural baggage in my family is _____

_____ .

6. Answer question 24 from page 104 of the textbook using the chart provided.

ETHNIC GROUP (ITALIAN, GERMAN, ETC.)	CULTURAL BAGGAGE

A CASE STUDY: MICHAEL PRYSZLAK

In 1922 Michael Pryszlak (pronounced *Prislak*) was born in the village of Bortiatyn in the Ukraine. Bortiatyn is not far from the city of L'vov in West Ukraine. Everyone in the village was of Ukrainian background, and most worked as farmers on nearby land. Bortiatyn had no electricity, no running water, and no cars. As a boy, Michael would help bring water to his family from community wells, as other children did in the village. In the wintertime, villagers had to walk to the river and chop a hole in the ice to get a bucket of water.

Michael's dad had three cows, two horses, and a vegetable garden, which supplied most of the family's food. There was not much free time to play since there were always chores to be done. Even the bread was baked at home in an old wood stove. Besides the bread a typical meal would include soup, beans, cabbage, and forest mushrooms. Four to five times a year Michael's family would have a treat — meat for dinner.

World War II

As the late 1930s approached, everyone in and around Bortiatyn sensed that war was approaching. In 1939 Michael left his village to look for work in L'vov. But within two years the Nazi army had moved into the Western Ukraine. There was little work or food in L'vov for Michael, so he took an offer to go to Germany to work. Originally the work offer was for three months. Soon the work period stretched into several years. The chance to return to the Ukraine soon disappeared.

When in Halle, Germany, he worked on the railroad for little pay and poor food. Michael found he was hungry all the time, living on just thin soup and a few slices of rotten bread. One night, as most others did, he stole a packet of biscuits to eat to stop the constant aching of hunger. Unfortunately a guard caught him and Michael ended up in prison for 18 months. While there he was assigned to hard labour on the railway.

After prison, he worked in a factory until the end of the war. In 1945 American troops moved through to free Michael and others who had been working in that part of Europe.

Search for a New Life

Michael had met his wife in 1943 but was only able to marry her in 1945, just before the end of the war. Through luck and help from a few friends the Pryszlaks were able to make their way through war-torn Europe to West Germany. For several years they applied to various countries as immigrants. France and the U.S.A. turned them down, but Canada accepted Michael only. In 1948 Michael came to Canada on a work permit and later was joined by his wife, Maria, and his daughter, Julie.

When Michael first arrived in Halifax he had only 55 cents in his pocket. He had to find a place to live, learn English, and find a long-term job. In addition he had to overcome discrimination against him as an immigrant. Today Michael lives in his own home with three children, Julie, Michael, and Bohdan.

The Pryszlaks still practise their Catholic religion and speak Ukrainian at home. They prepare much of their food in the traditional Ukrainian way and follow a number of Old World holiday traditions.

Sometimes when Michael thinks back to his childhood, he is amazed at how his life has changed. What personal freedom he has in Canada today! He hopes we never lose that freedom.

1. **(a)** Describe the village of Bortiatyn in the Ukraine. _____

_____

_____

   (b) In what four ways is Bortiatyn different from the area in which you

live? _____

_____

_____

2. Why was World War II such a difficult time for Michael Pryszlak? _____

_____

_____

_____

3. **(a)** What push factors encouraged the Pryszlaks to leave Europe? _____

_____

_____

   (b) What pull factor(s) brought the Pryszlaks to Canada? _____

_____

_____

_____

4. List five obstacles Michael had to overcome when he arrived in Canada.

   (a) _____

   (b) _____

   (c) _____

   (d) _____

   (e) _____

5. Have the Pryszlaks brought any cultural baggage along with them? _____
If yes, describe it. _____

_____

_____

6. Imagine for a moment that you are Michael Pryszlak. Why would you value
your personal freedom so much? _____

_____

_____

_____

_____

_____

_____

_____

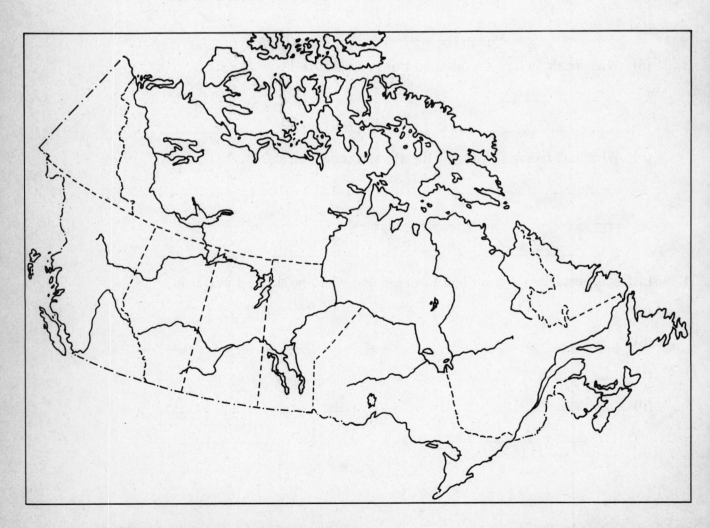

IMMIGRATION TO CANADA

1. On the blank map of Canada on page 108, answer question 30 (a) from page 107 of the textbook.

p. 107

2. Answer question 31 (b) on page 108 of the textbook, using the map on the next page.

p. 108

3. How does Canada receive valuable citizens "free"?

p. 109

_____

_____

4. What is a landed immigrant? _____

_____

5. What is Canadian citizenship and what five conditions must be met to obtain it?

p. 110

_____

_____

(a) _____

(b) _____

(c) _____

(d) _____

(e) _____

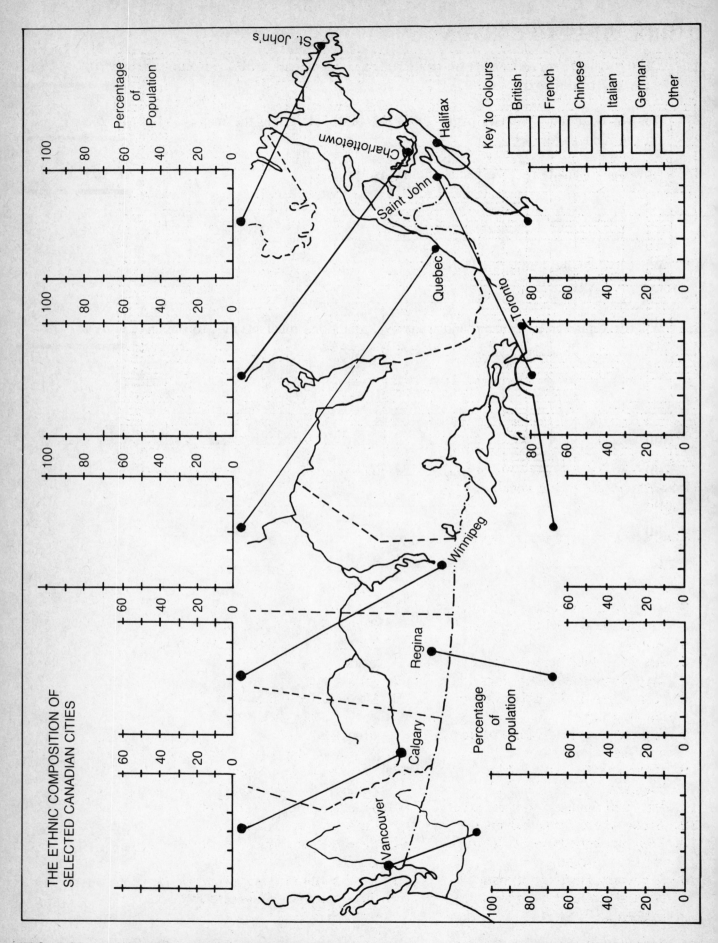

THE ETHNIC COMPOSITION OF
SELECTED CANADIAN CITIES

Key to Colours

British   French   Chinese   Italian   German   Other

Percentage
of
Population

Percentage
of
Population

VOCABULARY CROSSWORD

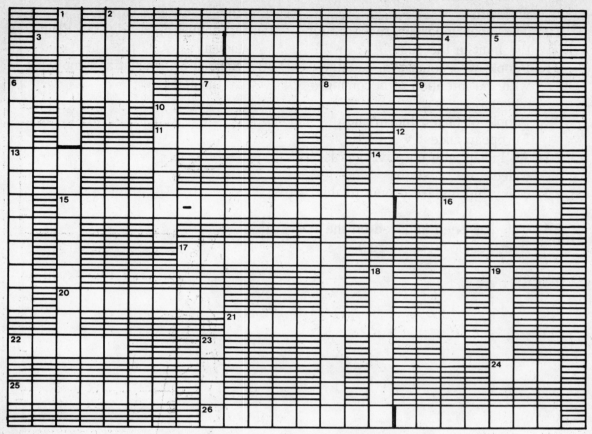

The answers are in the vocabulary on page 111 of the textbook and in Chapter 3.

Clues

ACROSS

3. It is the dream of many foreigners to become one of these. (two words)

4. An aid to Inuit transportation; they were dragged by dogs.

6. A member of the larger of our native groups

7. A dried food made from meat and cherries

9. "The people," in a native language

11. Dry material used to start fires

12. Areas where many Indians live

13. Most immigrants in St. John's are of _____ origin.

15. A country made up of many cultural groups (two words, one hyphenated)

DOWN

1. A person who has come to Canada and who will probably become a Canadian citizen. (two words)

2. An Inuit canoe

5. Most of our ancestors _____ from their native countries.

6. A type of ship vital in the Arctic

8. The traditions brought by immigrants (two words)

10. The Ukrainians are one of Canada's _____ groups.

14. Factors that attract people to Canada

16. Immigrants of this type make up three percent of Vancouver's population.

17. A kind of drink used to escape problems
20. The most important resource for the Inuit in the past
21. People who come to a country with the intention of becoming citizens
22. People of mixed Indian and European ancestry
24. An Indian with no privileges is called _____ -status
25. Many Indians are driven to this act.
26. This has been imposed on the Inuit people. (two words)

18. Toronto has the largest group of immigrants of this kind.
19. An animal hunted by the Plains Indians
23. A small plant used as lamp wick by the Inuit

WHERE WE LIVE

4

PERSONAL PROGRESS CHART

Put a check mark in the first square for each section when your teacher assigns it. When you have completed the section, put a check mark in the second square.

Page	Topic	Assigned by teacher	Completed by you
114	The Distribution of Canada's Population ___	☐	☐
114	Land Survey Systems		
114	Quebec _____	☐	☐
116	Ontario _____	☐	☐
117	Prairies _____	☐	☐
117	The Variety of Communities across Canada		
117	Farmsteads, Hamlets, and Villages ____	☐	☐
118	Towns and Ghost Towns _____	☐	☐
120	Cities _____	☐	☐
124	The Location of Cities _____	☐	☐
127	Rural-Urban Fringe _____	☐	☐
127	Megalopolis _____	☐	☐
128	Land Uses in a City _____	☐	☐
130	Urban Problems _____	☐	☐
134	Vocabulary Crossword _____	☐	☐

THE DISTRIBUTION OF CANADA'S POPULATION

p. 113

1. Circle either T (True) or F (False) for each of these statements.

(a) The majority of Canadians live in centres that are spread out over all of the country.　T　F

(b) The greatest concentration of population in Canada is along the shores of the Great Lakes and the St. Lawrence River.　T　F

(c) The inland valleys of the Maritime Provinces have almost no inhabitants.　T　F

(d) A thematic map is one that always shows the population of an area.　T　F

(e) Most Canadians live within 200 km of the U.S. border.　T　F

2. The location of the Canadian population influences what we watch on television because

_____

_____ .

LAND SURVEY SYSTEMS

Quebec

p. 114

1. The long lot system was centered on the _____ .

People preferred to live there because _____

_____ and

_____ .

The person who was responsible for first dividing up the land in Quebec

was called a _____ . The land he controlled was called

a _____ .

p. 115

2. Read question 5 (a), (b), and (c) at the top of page 115 in the textbook, and then fill in your answers on the sketch outlined below.

3. Answer question 5 (d) from page 115 on a blank piece of paper.

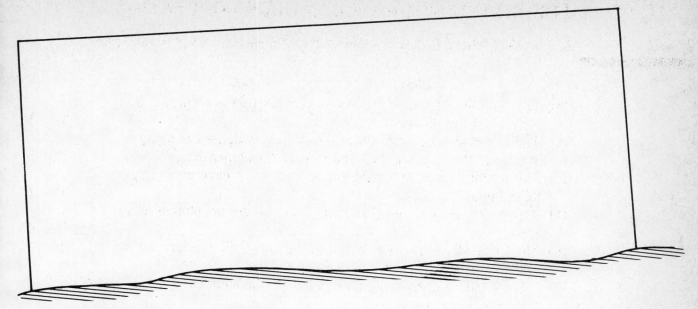

4. Complete the following diagram by

   (a) labelling it fully

   (b) shading in the first rang with one colour and the second rang with a
different colour

   (c) adding a third rang with houses and rotures.

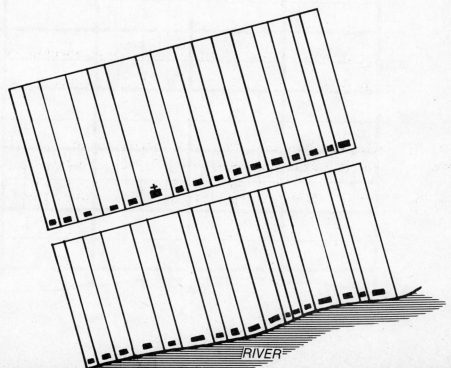

RIVER

Ontario

p. 116

1. Explain the meaning of each of these terms.

   (a) Surveying is _____

   _____ .

   (b) Base line is _____

   _____ .

   (c) A concession is _____

   _____ .

   (d) A concession line is _____ .

   (e) A side road is _____ .

p. 117

2. (a) Label the following diagram, based on Figure 4-4 on page 117 of the textbook.

THE SYSTEM OF SURVEYING IN AN ONTARIO TOWNSHIP

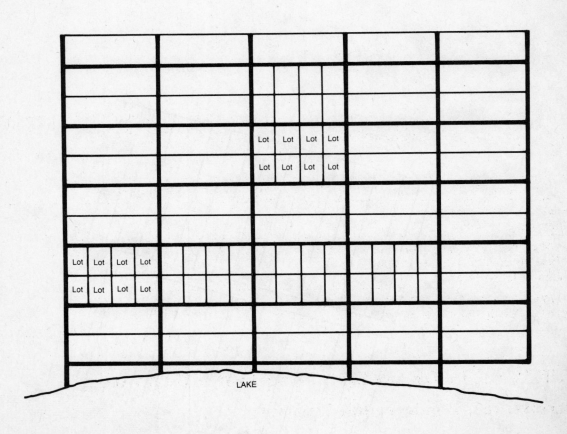

(b) Select two concessions and mark the location where houses would probably have been built.

3. The shape of lots in Ontario had advantages over the shape of lots in Quebec because

_____

_____ .

The Prairies

1. **(a)** Using the square, answer question 10 at the top of page 118 in the textbook.

p. 118

(b) A section is _____

_____ .

Compared to farms in other areas of

Canada, Prairie farms are _____ .

2. Complete the chart below, taken from page 119 in the textbook.

REGIONS OF CANADA	QUEBEC	ONTARIO	PRAIRIES
Distance of farmhouse from neighbours			
A square-shaped farm is most efficient to work. How efficient is each of these farms?			
How easy is the survey system to set up, relative to the others?			

THE VARIETY OF COMMUNITIES ACROSS CANADA

Farmsteads, Hamlets, and Villages

1. A farmstead is a _____ that provides such basic

services as _____ , _____ , and

_____ .

p. 120
2. Another term to describe a hamlet is _____ .

3. A few hamlets grew to become _____ . There are

_____ of villages across our country, each one with

possibly _____ people.

4. Map out a village on the map that follows. Include the features and land uses listed below the map. Use the symbols on page 44 of the textbook and locate them in suitable places in your village. Label particular buildings such as stores. Include a key.

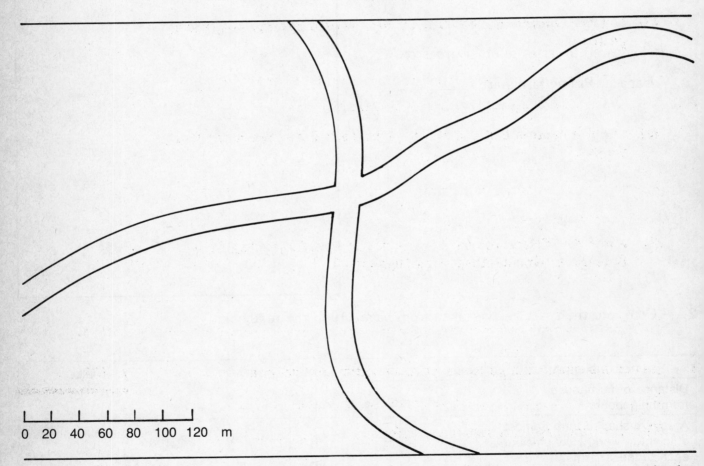

0 20 40 60 80 100 120 m

Features and Land Uses: 25 houses, 2 churches, one cemetery, a school, a gas station, a railway, a swamp, 2 towers, a post office, a small river and bridge, 4 stores, a bakery, and a restaurant.

Towns and Ghost Towns

p. 121
1. A town is _____ .

Major cities such as _____ and _____

were towns at one time.

2. Examine Figure 4-12 in your textbook and answer these questions.   *p. 122*

  (a) How many swimming beaches are shown on the map? _____

  (b) How many locations are there for boating facilities? _____

  (c) If you travelled from Nash Creek to Nigadoo, what settlements would

     you pass through? _____

     _____

     _____

  (d) List five centres that you believe were settled by English-speaking
     people.

     _____   _____   _____

     _____   _____

  (e) List five centres that you believe were settled by French-speaking
     people.

     _____   _____   _____

     _____   _____

  (f) Name the villages you would pass through when travelling from
     Bathurst to Grande-Anse along Highway 11.

     _____

     _____

3. Just as a business can go bankrupt, so a settlement can lose   *p. 123*

  its _____ and become a _____ .

  The economic base of a settlement includes _____

  _____ .

  Barkerville, B.C., was a settlement that was established

  _____

  because _____

  _____ .

  Unfortunately, soon _____

and left Barkerville a ghost town. From Figure 4-13, state the main

function for Barkerville today._____

Explain how you can tell this. _____

_____

Cities

p. 124

1. A city is a centre with at least _____ people living in it.

    Most Canadians live in _____ of

    _____ . Each city provides _____ and

    _____ for _____ as well as

    _____ .

2. Examine the following list. Decide on the basis of population only whether
    each centre is a hamlet, village, town, or city.

Population	Hamlet, Village, Town, or City
70 000	_____
25	_____
300	_____
5 000	_____
12	_____
276 000	_____
425	_____
3 000	_____
9 900	_____
1 000 000	_____

3. (a) Using the statistics given below, construct your own line graph, similar to Figure 4-14 in the textbook.

Percentage of the Canadian Population Living in Cities of over 100 000 Persons.

YEAR	PERCENTAGE
1871	3.1
1881	3.3
1891	8.2
1901	8.9
1911	15.0
1921	18.9
1931	22.4
1941	23.0
1951	23.3
1961	22.8
1971	26.7
1981	30.1

TITLE: _____

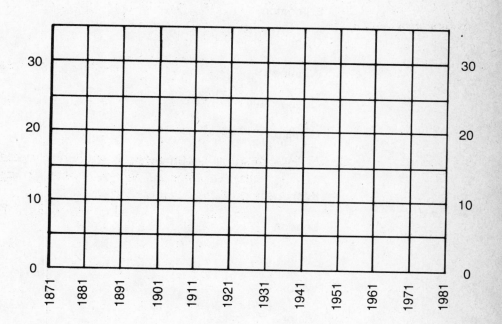

Many cities have increased their total populations by including surrounding urban areas. They have a central government that is beneficial in the running and organization of the whole area. These larger areas are called *Metropolitan Regions*, but for the sake of simplicity, they are just called ''cities'' here.

(b) During which ten-year period did the percentage of Canadians in cities of 100 000 or more increase the most? _____

How does this appear on the graph? _____

_____

(c) During which ten-year period did the percentage change the least? (Do not include a decrease.) _____

How is this reflected on the graph? _____

_____

CANADIAN CITIES HAVING OVER 100 000 PEOPLE (1985)

City	Population
Toronto	3 202 400
Montreal	2 878 200
Vancouver	1 348 600
Ottawa–Hull	769 900
Edmonton	683 600
Calgary	625 600
Winnipeg	612 100
Quebec City	593 500
Hamilton	559 700
St. Catharines–Niagara Falls	309 400
Kitchener	303 400
London	292 700
Halifax	290 600
Windsor	249 800
Victoria	245 100
Regina	174 800
Oshawa	172 800
Saskatoon	170 100
St. John's, Newfoundland	160 700
Sudbury	147 600
Chicoutimi–Jonquière	139 400
Thunder Bay	123 500
Saint John, New Brunswick	116 800
Trois Rivières	114 300

4. List the provinces in order, according to the number of cities they have that are over 100 000 in population. Write in the number of cities in each province. Count Ottawa as one and Hull as another.

(a) _____
(largest number)

(f) _____

(b) _____

(g) _____

(c) _____

(h) _____

(d) _____

(i) _____

(e) _____

(j) _____
(smallest number)

5. Add up the populations of the ten largest Canadian cities, and then carry out this calculation. (Use the space provided to do your rough work. In 1985 Canada's population was 25 444 900.)

$$\frac{\text{Sum of population in 10 largest cities}}{\text{(population of Canada)}} \times \frac{100}{1}$$

$$= \underline{\hspace{2cm}} \times \frac{100}{1}$$

$$= \underline{\hspace{2cm}} \%$$

This is the percentage of Canadians who live in Canada's ten largest cities.

6. **(a)** On the accompanying map of Canada, mark and label the Canadian cities whose populations are over 100 000. You will need your atlas. The map is on page 124.

(b) Join each city to the ones nearest to it, using straight lines to represent highways. Compare this pattern of roads to that found in your atlas.

What differences can you detect between the two? _____

_____

Give reasons for these differences where possible. _____

_____

_____

THE LOCATION OF CITIES

p. 127

1. Using your atlas to help you, describe the locations of the cities listed below, relative to bodies of water. The first city is completed for you as an example.

CITY	BODY (OR BODIES) OF WATER IT IS NEARBY	DESCRIPTION OF ITS LOCATION
Vancouver	Pacific Ocean and Fraser River	At mouth of Fraser River
Halifax		
Montreal		

Toronto		
Calgary		
Winnipeg		
Thunder Bay		
Saint John		

2. (a) A break-of-bulk point is _____

_____ .

(b) Hinterland means _____

_____ .

3. Sketch a diagram to illustrate a break-of-bulk point. Use Figure 4-18 from your textbook as a guide.

4. Canadian cities tend to be located according to five principles:

    (a) Urban areas tend to be located _____

_____ .

    (b) Essentially, urban centres are _____ for the

surrounding land.

    (c) Some centres have _____ .

    (d) A number of large Canadian cities serve as _____

or _____ .

    (e) For any centre to be founded, someone _____ at

some time in the past.

5. Contrast site and situation by explaining the meaning of each.

SITE	SITUATION
_____	_____
_____	_____
_____	_____
_____	_____

6. Answer question 33 on page 129 of the textbook by filling in the following chart.

SITE	ACCEPT OR REJECT	REASONS FOR ACCEPTING OR REJECTING IT
A		
B		
C		
D		
E		

RURAL-URBAN FRINGE

1. Around Canadian cities there is an area of land that is neither a built-up city nor a farming area. This area is referred to as _____ .

p. 131

2. To avoid land uses that are in conflict, most Canadian cities have set up _____ . These specify where _____ .

p. 133

3. Urban planning refers to _____ .

4. Property taxes are collected from _____ and provide money for services such as _____

_____ .

MEGALOPOLIS

1. A megalopolis is _____ .

p. 133

In Canada there is an area in which a megalopolis is actually beginning to form. This area is _____ .

2. Turn in your atlas to a map of southern Ontario. Mark and label on the map below the cities that could be included in a megalopolis.

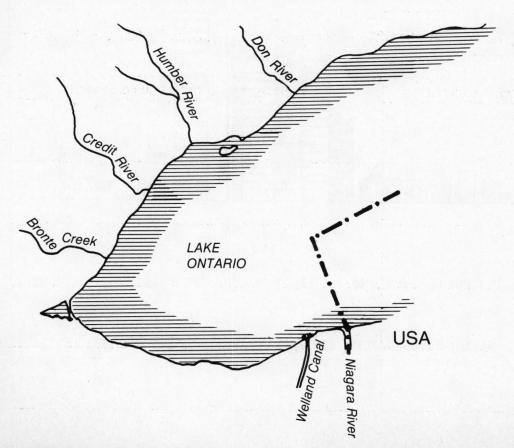

LAND USES IN A CITY

1. Match each term in the left column with the most correct explanation of its meaning in the right column.

Redevelopment _____ •

Residential land use _____ •

Central business district _____ •

Industrial land use _____ •

Commercial land use _____ •

• Factories and manufacturing are

• Downtown area with tallest offi

• Where people shop and conduct their business

• Where people live

• Tearing down old buildings and replacing them with new buildin

2. On the skyline below, draw a large circle around the area of the city that you believe is the central business district.

p. 135

3. In cities people live in the type of housing they either _____

or can _____ .

p. 136

4. **(a)** On this map, mark and label the two likely locations for high-income housing and two possible locations for low-income residential area

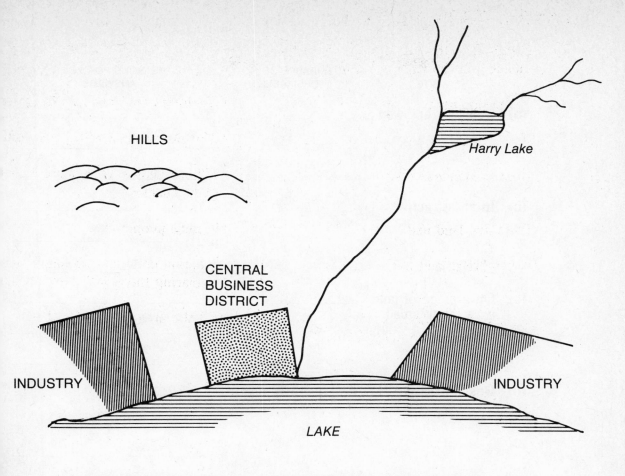

HILLS

CENTRAL
BUSINESS
DISTRICT

Harry Lake

INDUSTRY

INDUSTRY

LAKE

(b) I located the high-income housing in this particular place

because _____

_____ .

(c) The low-income housing was located in this particular place

because _____

_____ .

5. Scattered throughout the residential areas are _____

land uses, such as _____ .

6. Industry can be described as the _____ *p. 137*

_____ .

This is true because it provides _____

_____ and pays _____

_____ .

7. Which of the following would be desirable sites for industry? Give reasons for your answers.

SITE	DESIRABLE OR NOT DESIRABLE	REASONS FOR YOUR ANSWERS
(a) Beside a highway	_____	_____
		_____
		_____
(b) In an attractive hilly area of a city	_____	_____
		_____
		_____
(c) On a piece of land with many small streams and valleys	_____	_____
		_____
		_____
(d) Beside a large lake	_____	_____
		_____
		_____

8. Explain the meaning of industrial park.

_____

_____

9. The centre of shopping in Canadian cities has been the

_____ .

Two other locations are common for shopping by Canadians; these

are _____ and _____ .

URBAN PROBLEMS

pp. 138-139

1. Cities provide many benefits but also have a number of significant problems. List three problems found in cities.

(a) _____

(b) _____

(c) _____

Research

2. Answer question 48 on page 138 in the textbook. Use the chart below for your answers.

p. 138

TYPE OF PROBLEM	CRIME	POLLUTION	TRAFFIC PROBLEMS	OTHER PROBLEMS
Specific description of problems (for example: theft, accident)				
Possible solutions (If no ideas are contained in the newspaper article, make your own suggestion.)				

3. From your own experience in visiting or living in cities, what problems bother you? Using correct sentence form, write a third of a page to describe these problems.

_____

_____

_____

_____

_____

_____

_____

_____

Mystery Cities in Canada

From the descriptions given below, discover the correct Canadian city and answer the questions to follow. Use your atlas to help out.

Mystery City No. 1:

(a) On one of the Great Lakes
(b) Large harbour
(c) Sometimes called "Steel City"
(d) Population of over 500 000

This city is _____ .

Describe its situation. _____

_____

What other industries does it have? _____

_____

_____

Mystery City No. 2:

(a) Capital of a province
(b) Not far from the Swan Hills
(c) No major Canadian city is further north
(d) Plenty of oil found nearby

This city is _____ .

Describe the situation of this city, especially with respect to North America as a whole.

_____

_____

In what two ways could this city be considered a "Gateway to the North"?

(i) _____

(ii) _____

Mystery City No. 3:

(a) On the Atlantic Ocean
(b) The province it is in does not touch the land area of the United States
(c) An important port
(d) It is not on an island

This city is _____ .

What transportation connections does this city have with the rest of Canada?

_____

Is it well located in its province to be a capital city? _____

Explain. _____

_____

Mystery City No. 4:

(a) Population between 100 000 and 200 000
(b) Between 200 and 400 mm of precipitation per year
(c) Downstream from the Gardiner Dam
(d) Located on a river named after its province

This city is _____ .

Describe the situation of this city. _____

_____

Which cities are linked to this city by highway? _____

_____

VOCABULARY CROSSWORD

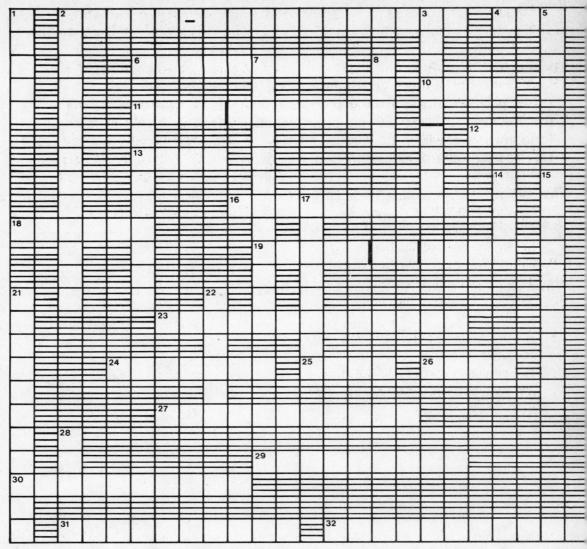

The answers are in the vocabulary on page 143 of the textbook and in Chapter 4.

Clues

ACROSS

2. The area where the city is spreading into the countryside (two words, one hyphenated)

4. The name of the area of one farm in Quebec

6. An area of land in Quebec, subdivided into farms

10. The land on which a city is built

11. The smallest settlement (two words)

12. Smaller than a town

DOWN

1. Businesses along a road make up a commercial _____ .

2. Removing old buildings and replacing them with new ones

3. A deserted town (two words)

5. When a village grows, it becomes a _____ .

7. The money-earning activities in an area (two words)

8. The _____ line is the first line that is surveyed.

13. A side _____ is built at right angles to concession roads in Ontario.
16. The land behind a port, served by that port
18. Another word for "four corners"
19. A town where goods are loaded and unloaded (three words)
23. Money that all homeowners have to pay (two words)
24. The basic survey area in the Prairies
25. Toronto is the _____ with the highest population in Canada.
26. A concession _____ is drawn between two concessions.
27. Cities that have grown together
29. The location of a town
30. The _____ zone has noise and traffic.
31. A strip of land parallel to the baseline
32. Hospitals, schools, and libraries are examples of this type of land use.

9. The person in charge of a seigneury
11. Another name for a farm
14. Many factories are located in an industrial _____ .
15. Shops, offices, and banks are located in _____ areas.
17. Maps of climate, soils, and vegetation are of this type.
20. Measuring the land to make maps
21. The zone where houses are built
22. By-laws that control building types in an area
28. Central business district

5 FARMING IN CANADA

PERSONAL PROGRESS CHART

Put a check mark in the first square for each section when your teacher assigns it. When you have completed the section, put a check mark in the second square.

Page	Topic	Assigned by teacher	Completed by you
137	Quiz	☐	☐
137	Clearing the Forest	☐	☐
141	Changes in Canadian Farming	☐	☐
143	The Importance of Agriculture	☐	☐
144	Distribution of Different Types of Agriculture in Canada	☐	☐
145	Wheat Farming	☐	☐
146	Ranching	☐	☐
147	Dairying	☐	☐
149	Orchards	☐	☐
150	Market Gardening	☐	☐
152	Tobacco	☐	☐
153	Mixed Farming	☐	☐
154	Distribution of Canada's Food Land	☐	☐
156	Government Programs to Help Poor Farmers	☐	☐
157	Vocabulary Crossword	☐	☐

QUIZ

1. Read the quiz on pages 146 to 147 of the textbook. Record your answers — (a), (b), (c), or (d) — in the column provided. *pp. 146-147*

Question	My Answer	Correct Answer (write out in full)
(a) The value of an average farm in Canada is near	....	
(b) The largest farms in Canada, on the average, are found in	....	
(c) For a broiler chicken to gain 1 kg, it must consume	....	
(d) Of each dollar that you spend on food, how much does the farmer receive?	....	
(e) What percentage of Canada's total area is farmland?	....	
(f) For a cow to gain 1 kg it must eat	....	
(g) Which province has the largest area of farmland in Canada?	....	
(h) In which province has the most farmland been abandoned in the past 25 years?	....	
(i) Each Canadian farmer, on average, produces enough food to support	....	
(j) As a result of serious drought (lack of rainfall) in the Prairies in the 1930s, how many Prairie farmers abandoned their land?	....	
TOTAL CORRECT _____		

2. Now check the answers on page 179 of the text. Mark your answers and write in the correct answers in full in the right-hand column.

   If you had 7 to 10 correct, you are an agricultural whiz.
   If you scored 4 to 6, you have done better than most.
   A score of 0 to 3 shows that you are not a good guesser!

CLEARING THE FOREST

1. Read page 147 of the textbook, and look at the photographs and drawing on page 148. *p. 147*

(a) What methods did the pioneers use to clear the forest? _____

_____

_____

(b) Describe two kinds of land that should not be cleared for agriculture. Give reasons for each of your choices.

    (i) _____ should not be cleared because _____

    _____ .

    (ii) _____ should not be cleared because _____

    _____ .

A Pioneer's Problem

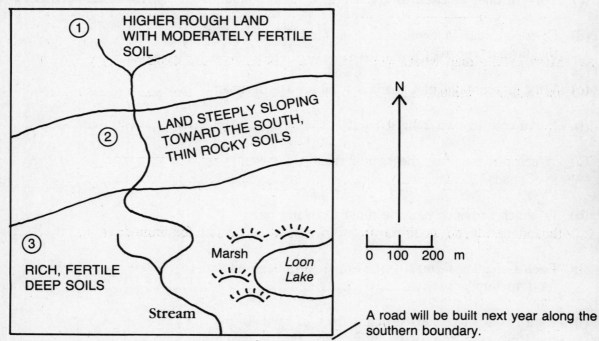

A road will be built next year along the southern boundary.

Imagine that, in March of 1832, you, your wife or husband, and three young children have just bought the land shown by the map. The land is located in southern Canada. All the land is heavily forested.

In order to survive you must provide yourselves with
    a temporary shelter for the summer
    a warmer home for the winter
    food and water supplies for now and later.

You already have
    a horse and wagon
    a 6 × 8 m piece of canvas
    one large cooking pot and two smaller ones
    a few kitchen utensils (spoons, plates, and so on)
    a barrel of flour and some yeast

5 kg of fat
two axes and one cross-cut saw
20 kg of salt pork
a rifle and a supply of ammunition
20 kg of dried beans
a cow and two sheep
five blankets
a small amount of money.

1. Describe how you would construct a temporary shelter. _____

_____

_____

_____

_____

2. Mark on the map where you would put this shelter and explain why you

chose this location. _____

_____

_____

_____

3. Explain what you would do to provide food and water for immediate use.

_____

_____

_____

4. What land would you choose to clear first? Mark this on the map and

explain why you chose that area first. _____

_____

_____

5. **(a)** Design your own winter house. Draw the plan of the rooms and label
   them. Draw a picture of the front of the house. Remember to give a
   scale to show the size of your home. Remember that it will have to be
   small and *simple*; it will also need a fireplace.

Plan of Rooms (seen from above)	Front View

(b) What materials will you use for the walls, windows, fireplace, and roof of your house? _____

_____

_____

_____

(c) Mark your house on the map. Why did you choose this place?

_____

_____

(d) What will you do for your toilet? Where will it be? _____

_____

(e) Explain what improvements you will make to your house in the next two years. _____

_____

_____

(f) What preparations must you make for the winter? _____

_____

_____

_____

_____

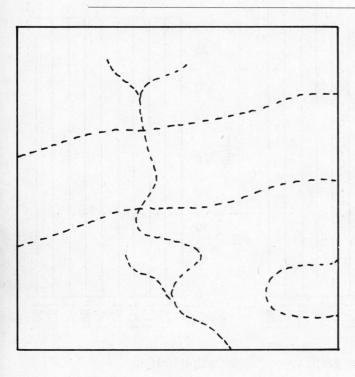

(g) Show how you will have developed your farm after ten years have passed. On the map, show all the buildings, roads and paths, vegetable gardens, fields, grazing land, forested areas, and so on. Use a key for colours and symbols.

THE FARM AFTER TEN YEARS OF HARD WORK

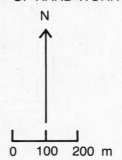

0   100   200 m

CHANGES IN CANADIAN FARMING

1. Fill in the blanks.

p. 149

The percentage of Canada's population working on farms is _____

_____ . _____ people are now

needed to produce food than in the past. At the same time as the farm

population has been declining, the food production from Canadian farms has

been _____ _____ . This means

that the _____ of Canadian farms has been improving,

since _____ farmers produce _____

_____ .

2. Using Figure 5-4, answer question 3 at the bottom of page 149 of the textbook.

CHANGES IN TECHNOLOGY ON CANADIAN FARMS

① Workers/kha*

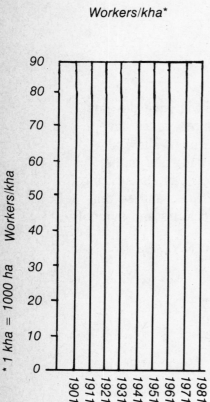

② Fertilizer (t/kha)**

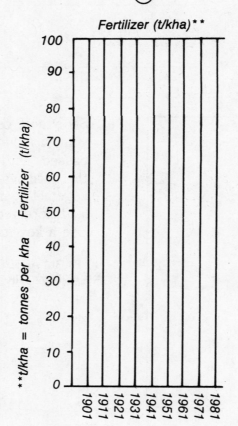

③ Machines/kha

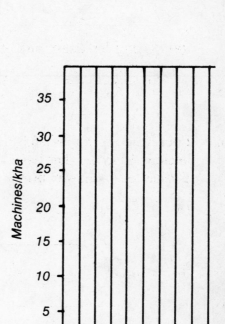

3. What is shown by the three graphs you have completed?

(a) Graph 1 shows _____

_____ .

(b) Graph 2 shows _____

_____ .

(c) Graph 3 shows _____

_____

pp. 150-151

4. Looking at the graphs you have drawn, Figure 5-5 on page 150 in your textbook, and the photographs on page 151, describe the ways in which the farmer's life has changed.

(a) Ploughing the land _____

_____

(b) Sowing seeds _____
_____

(c) Raising poultry _____
_____

(d) Harvesting _____
_____

(e) Using fertilizers and other chemical products _____
_____
_____

5. Look at your graphs and Figure 5-5 once more. Name four industries, besides farming, that have benefited from farming changes since 1850. Explain each answer briefly.

(a) _____
_____

(b) _____
_____

(c) _____
_____

(d) _____
_____

THE IMPORTANCE OF AGRICULTURE

1. Read the section in the centre of page 152 in the textbook. List and briefly explain three reasons why agriculture is very important to Canada.

p. 152

(a) _____
_____

(b) _____
_____

(c) _____
_____

From the Farm to Your Table

pp. 152-153

1. Imagine that on three separate occasions you go into your local food store to buy carrots.

    (a) In the winter, you need some canned carrots to put into a stew. What parts of the food marketing system, shown on page 153 in Figure 5-6 of your textbook, would those canned carrots pass through on their way to your home from the farm?

    FARM — _____ — _____ — _____ — _____ — HOME

    (b) In the summer, you buy some fresh carrots for a salad. Through which stages would the carrots have passed?

    FARM — _____ — _____ — HOME

    (c) In the fall, you buy stored carrots for a vegetable. What stages would those carrots have passed through?

    FARM — _____ — _____ — _____ — HOME

2. Why do we use chemical preservatives in so many of our foods? _____

    _____

    _____

DISTRIBUTION OF DIFFERENT TYPES OF AGRICULTURE IN CANADA

p. 154

1. What two factors are very important in determining the types of crops

    that are grown? _____ and _____

2. In intensive farming, the farms are usually quite _____

    and require much _____ to operate. Two examples are

    _____ and _____ farming.

    In extensive farming, farms are usually very _____

    and involve less _____ . Two examples of extensive

    farming are _____ and _____ .

3. **(a)** Look at the maps on pages 113 and 154 in the textbook. What relationship is there between the agricultural areas of Canada and the population distribution?

    _____

    _____

(b) Why do you think that this relationship exists?

_____

_____

4. Look carefully at Figure 5-7 on page 154 in the textbook. Circle the correct answers.

(a) In which province would you find most of the farms that concentrate on wheat growing?
• Alberta • Saskatchewan • Ontario • British Columbia

(b) The agricultural activity that covers the smallest area is
• cattle ranching   • grain and livestock
• fruit, vegetables, tobacco   • mixed farming

(c) Most dairy farms would be found in
• Ontario and Quebec   • Prince Edward Island
• Manitoba   • British Columbia

(d) The type of agriculture that extends farthest north is
• wheat growing   • fruit growing
• vegetables and livestock   • mixed farming, grain, and
                                             livestock

WHEAT FARMING

1. Why are the Prairie Provinces called the "bread basket of Canada"?   *p. 155*

_____

2. List three reasons why the Prairie land is so well suited for wheat growing.

(a) _____

(b) _____

(c) _____

3. **(a)** What is involved in dryland farming? _____

_____

(b) Why is dryland farming used in some parts of the Prairies?

_____

_____

4. Use lines to connect wheat-growing problems with solutions.

PROBLEMS	SOLUTIONS
weeds •	• new strains
disease •	• no solution
insects •	• herbicides
early snowfall •	• pesticides

p. 156

5. Imagine that your job is to choose the best routes for exporting Prairie wheat. In the table below, put a check mark under the name of the ports you would consider using. Circle the best choice. Briefly explain why you chose that route. One example is done for you.

	Prince Rupert	Vancouver	Churchill	Thunder Bay	Toronto	Montreal	(PREFERRED ROUTE)
January: to Asia							
to Europe	✔	✔				⊘	Closer (others frozen)
July: to Asia							
to Europe							

Refer to Figure 5-9 on page 156 of your textbook to help with your answer.

RANCHING

p. 158

1. Why are horses so important in modern ranching?

_____

_____

2. In which two provinces is large-scale ranching important? _____

and _____

3. What is the name of Canada's largest rodeo? _____

_____

How often does it occur? _____ Name the kinds of

activities at the rodeo. _____

_____

4. In Alberta, what are the ranch areas like? _____

_____

5. In British Columbia, ranches are concentrated in the _____

Plateau, which is much _____ than near Calgary.

6. **(a)** What is meant by transhumance?_____ *p. 159*

_____

   (b) Fill in the following diagram using Figure 5-12 on page 159 of
   the textbook.

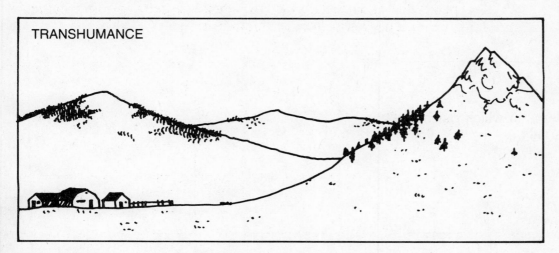

TRANSHUMANCE

7. How do farmers prepare cattle before slaughter? _____

_____

DAIRYING

1. Which dairy products do you eat or drink? Look at Figure 5-14 on page *p. 160*
160 of your textbook for some ideas.

_____

_____

2. **(a)** What is meant by industrial milk? _____

_____

   (b) Which province produces most of our industrial milk? _____

3. Which province produces most of our fluid milk? _____

Operating a Dairy Farm

pp. 161-162   1.   Read the description of how a dairy farm is run.

(a) Briefly explain three reasons why dairy farming is more demanding than wheat farming.

(i) _____

_____

(ii) _____

_____

(iii) _____

_____

(b) Give two ways in which ranching and dairying differ.

(i) _____

_____

_____

_____

_____

_____

(ii) _____

_____

_____

_____

_____

_____

100 m

| 1 ha |

1 cm rep 100 m
1 cm² rep 1 ha

Road

2. Read the description of Mr. Cooke's dairy farm on pages 161 and 162 of the textbook. Answer question 20 (c) on page 162.

ORCHARDS

1. Name the four major fruit-growing areas in Canada (include the names of the provinces where they are located).

p. 163

_____   _____

_____   _____

2. Each of these fruit areas has special climate and soil characteristics.

(a) What is special about the climate? _____

_____

(b) What are the soils like? _____

_____

3. Copy the wheel diagram from page 164 in the textbook.

p. 164

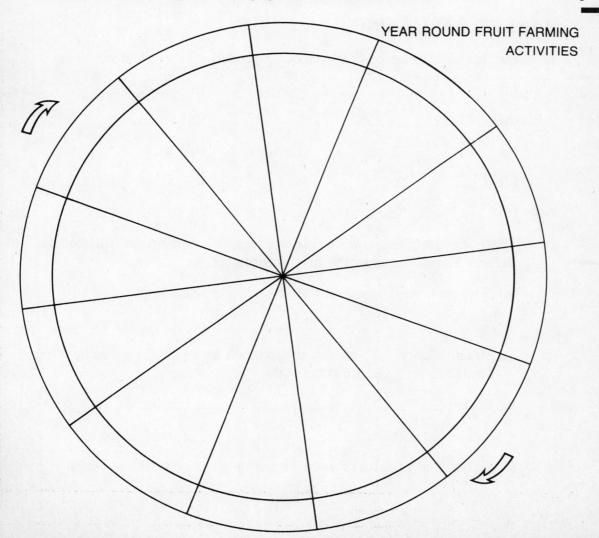

YEAR ROUND FRUIT FARMING
ACTIVITIES

4. Look at the photographs on pages 164 and 165 of your textbook. Answer these questions.

(a) On page 164, what do they call the process of cutting twigs

from a tree? _____

Why do you think that it is done? _____

_____

(b) On page 164, why are the workers bothering to pick up the twigs?

_____

_____

(c) On page 165, top left, what is the big machine doing?_____

_____

Why is this necessary?_____

MARKET GARDENING

p. 170

1. List ten different crops that might be produced by market gardening.

(a) _____ (f) _____

(b) _____ (g) _____

(c) _____ (h) _____

(d) _____ (i) _____

(e) _____ (j) _____

p. 167

2. There are many areas in Canada where such crops are grown, but the Holland Marsh is one of the most interesting.

(a) Describe what the area was like about 60 years ago.

_____

_____

(b) Using Figure 5-23 from your textbook as a guide, explain how excess water is removed from the soil.

_____

_____

p. 169

(c) What kind of settlers were encouraged to come to the Marsh

in 1931? _____

Why were they encouraged? _____

_____

3. Answer questions 31 and 32 on page 170 in the textbook.

p. 170

   (31) **(a)** In 1954 _____ covered the most land.

       (b) _____ occupied _____ percent of the

       land in 1985.

   (32) **(a)** The most important crops in the Holland Marsh today are

       _____ and _____.

       (b) These two crops give a more dependable, year-round income for

       the farmers because _____

       _____.

4. Construct two bar graphs as directed in question 33 on page 170 in the textbook. Use the accompanying graph for your answer.

Percentages

CHANGING PERCENTAGES
OF PRODUCTION OF CROPS IN
HOLLAND MARSH

1954   1985

5. How long will Holland Marsh remain productive? _____

p. 171

6. When this land goes out of production, what will happen to the farmers?

_____

What will happen to the people of southern Ontario? _____

_____

7. What should be done to ensure a future supply of vegetables in Southern Ontario?_____

_____

TOBACCO

p. 171

1. Where are the main tobacco growing areas in Canada?

_____ , _____ , and _____

2. Why are people smoking fewer cigarettes?

   (a) _____

   (b) _____

3. List five kinds of activities or people who would be affected by the current crisis affecting the tobacco industry in Canada. Briefly explain how each has been affected.

   (a) _____

   (b) _____

   (c) _____

   (d) _____

   (e) _____

4. Use this space to construct the flow chart in question 36 on page 172 of the textbook.

5. The amount of tobacco which may be grown by each farmer is strictly controlled by local growers' associations. This amount is called a quota. (Egg and milk production are also controlled by quotas.) Quotas help to keep the value of the product high by restricting supply.

(a) What is a quota?_____

(b) What is the aim of quotas?_____

(c) Who benefits from quotas?_____ In what

ways?_____

6. Imagine that you are a member of a committee which has to report to the local growers' association. You are to make three suggestions which might improve the failing economy of the area and the life of the people who live there.

(a) _____

_____

(b) _____

_____

(c) _____

_____

MIXED FARMING

1. What is mixed farming?_____ *pp. 172-173*

_____

2. In what three ways can mixed farming be better for the farmer than specialized farming?

(a) _____

(b) _____

(c) _____

Farm Poverty

1. Explain what marginal farmland is. _____

_____

2. Look at Figure 5-31 on page 173 in the textbook. Explain why it is so difficult for a poor farmer to increase the value of the crops he produces. Start at "Poor crops."

_____

_____

_____

_____

_____

Locating a Farm

pp. 173-174

1. Answer question 42 on pages 173 and 174 in the textbook.
   (a) Draw your farm and the details of soil types and river (if included) in the square on the right.

   ⟵——1 km——⟶

   (b) My farm has the advantages of _____

   _____

   _____

   (c) I might meet problems in trying to farm the land I have chosen

   because _____

   _____

   _____

DISTRIBUTION OF CANADA'S FOOD LAND

p. 175

1. Look at Figure 5-33 on page 175 in your textbook and answer questions 44 and 45 below.

(a) Order of provinces, by area of farmland, largest first:

(i) _____ **(v)** _____ **(viii)** _____
(largest)

(ii) _____ **(vi)** _____ **(ix)** _____

(iii) _____ **(vii)** _____ **(x)** _____
(smallest)

(iv) _____

(b) The two provinces with the most agricultural land are

_____ and _____.

The five provinces with the least agricultural land are

_____, _____,

_____, _____, and

_____.

Those with intermediate amounts of agricultural land are

_____, _____, and

_____.

2.   **(a)** The province with the greatest proportion of poor land (classes

5 or 6) is _____.

(b) The province with the greatest area of the best land (class 1) is

_____.

(c) In provinces with much poor land,_____

_____.

In provinces with much good land,_____

_____.

THE PIONEER FRINGE

1.   Where is new land being opened up for farming today?_____ p. 176

2.   In what ways is the life of today's pioneer different from the ways of
pioneers 100 years ago?

_____

_____

_____

_____

3. Would you like to be a pioneer farmer? _____. Give at least four reasons for your answer.

_____

_____

_____

_____

GOVERNMENT PROGRAMS TO HELP POOR FARMERS

_p. 178_

1. What happens on an experimental farm?_____

_____

2. ARDA is sponsored by the _____ government. It

concentrates on _____ and _____

conservation, _____ of farmland, and assistance for

_____.

3. The Farm Improvements Loans Act helps farmers to get back

_____ of up to $ _____. These

loans must be repaid within _____, or 15 years, if

_____.

4. PFRA began during the serious _____ of the 1930s.

Its main aim is to _____

_____

_____.

VOCABULARY CROSSWORD

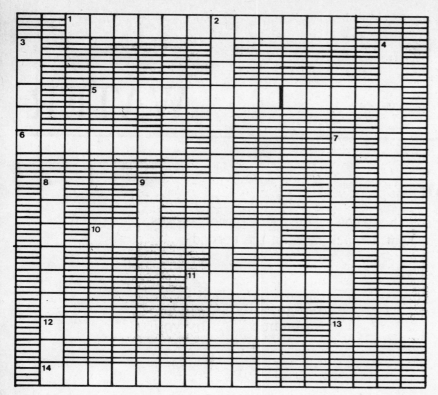

The answers are in the vocabulary on page 179 of the textbook and in Chapter 5.

Clues

ACROSS

1. The amount produced by one worker
5. ____ ____ kill soft fruits very easily. (two words)
6. Types of plants or animals
9. Troughs for irrigation water
10. Farmland of limited value
11. "Fattening farm" for cattle
12. Artificial watering
13. ____ icides kill weeds.
14. Farming in the Prairies is mainly ____.

DOWN

2. The seasonal movement of animals in mountainous areas
3. Pipes used to drain soil
4. Chemicals used to kill insects
7. A long, dry spell of weather
8. Farming that involves much labour

6

WATER

PERSONAL PROGRESS CHART

Put a check mark in the first square for each section when your teacher assigns it. When you have completed the section, put a check mark in the second square.

Page	Topic	Assigned by teacher	Completed by you
159	Water: An Introduction	☐	☐
160	Water Supply and Use in Canada	☐	☐
160	Hydrologic Cycle	☐	☐
162	The Importance of Precipitation	☐	☐
162	Water Run-off	☐	☐
163	The Variation in Seasonal Run-off	☐	☐
164	Groundwater	☐	☐
165	The Drainage Basin of a River	☐	☐
168	Water Surplus: Problems and Solutions	☐	☐
171	Water Deficit: Problems and Solutions	☐	☐
172	Water Management	☐	☐
176	Pollution	☐	☐
179	Vocabulary Crossword	☐	☐

WATER: AN INTRODUCTION

1. Water is vital to life on earth. To understand water's importance, match each item in the left column with the correct percentage of it that is water. Draw lines to connect each item with the correct percentage.

p. 182

ITEM	PERCENTAGE OF WATER
Your body _____•	90%
Edible fruits and vegetables _____•	10%-15%
Milk _____•	70%
Grains, dried peas, and beans _____•	50%-75%
Meats _____•	95%

2. Water can dissolve so many substances that it has been referred to as the

   _____ .

3. Circle the correct answers below, using the information on page 182 in your textbook.

   (a) Every day each person in an average Canadian household uses
   - 500 L water
   - 175 L water
   - 315 L water
   - 225 L water

   (b) One millilitre of water has a mass of
   - 100 g
   - 1 g
   - 10 g
   - 0.1 g

   (c) At sea level, water boils at
   - 90°C
   - 100°C
   - 200°C
   - 212°C

   (d) Water freezes at
   - 0°C
   - 10°C
   - –5°C
   - –100°C

WATER SUPPLY AND USE IN CANADA

p. 183

1. Canada is a unique country in terms of water supply. Describe its uniqueness under these headings.

   (a) Ocean shoreline _____

   _____

   (b) Total area of fresh water _____

   _____

   (c) Amount of fresh water per person _____

   _____

HYDROLOGIC CYCLE

p. 184

1. Label fully this diagram of the hydrologic cycle. Include the arrows. Use Figure 6-4 in your textbook to help you.

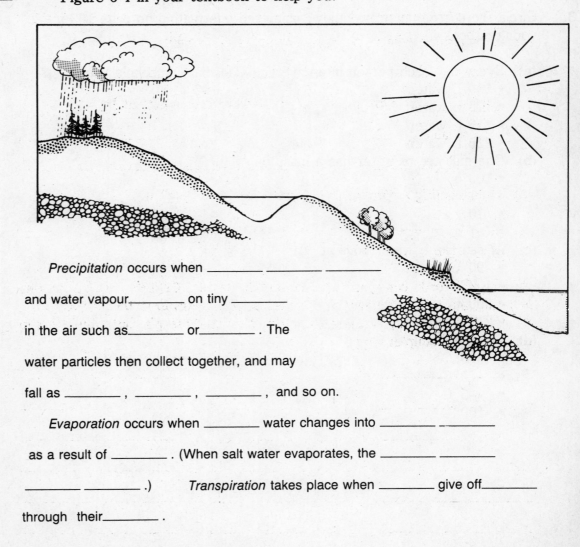

Precipitation occurs when _____ _____ _____

and water vapour_____ on tiny _____

in the air such as_____ or_____ . The

water particles then collect together, and may

fall as _____ , _____ , _____ , and so on.

Evaporation occurs when _____ water changes into _____ _____

as a result of _____ . (When salt water evaporates, the _____ _____

_____ _____ .) *Transpiration* takes place when _____ give off_____

through their_____ .

2. For each statement below, circle either T (True) or F (False).

    (a) Precipitation occurs when moist air cools and water vapour condenses on tiny particles in the air.   T   F

    (b) Transpiration and evaporation both add water vapour to the air.   T   F

    (c) Precipitation cannot take place unless evaporation and transpiration occur.   T   F

    (d) One reason why little precipitation occurs in the desert is that there are very few lakes for evaporation to take place.   T   F

    (e) Water vapour can be seen quite clearly and looks like fog.   T   F

    (f) When salt water evaporates, the salt in the air causes salty precipitation, which kills many trees.   T   F

3. Read question 6 on page 184 in the textbook and record your answers below.

    (a) Chopping down trees at A would _____

    _____

    _____ .

    (b) Draining the lake at B and the marsh at C would _____

    _____ .

    (c) Building a city with paved streets and large buildings at D

    would cause _____

    _____ .

    (d) Constructing a dam on the river at E would result in _____

    _____ .

4. WORD GAME

How many words can you make from HYDROLOGIC CYCLE? RULES: You can only use each letter as many times as it appears in HYDROLOGIC CYCLE. For example, you could use two *l*'s and three *c*'s, but only one *e* in each word. Example: clog

_____   _____   _____

_____   _____   _____

_____   _____   _____

_____   _____   _____

_____   _____   _____

Try to fill these spaces. If you have more words, use your own paper.

THE IMPORTANCE OF PRECIPITATION

p. 185

1. Summer maximum means_____

_____ .

Winter maximum, in contrast, means _____

_____

2. For each climograph below, complete only the bars for precipitation for the year. Use any amounts of precipitation you want, as long as the maximum occurs at the correct season. Use page 54 in your textbook to review climographs.

Draw in precipitation bars to show:

(a) A summer maximum   **(b)** A winter maximum   **(c)** No distinct seasonal maximum

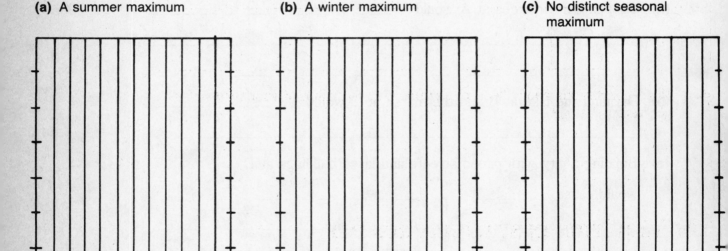

WATER RUN-OFF

p. 186

1. What is run-off? _____

_____

2. Approximately _____% of all precipitation in Canada ends up as run-off.

Snow that falls in winter does not add to run-off until _____ .

This process occurs more slowly in forests than _____

because _____ .

3. Read question 10 (a) on page 186 in the textbook and record your answers below.

SITES (RANK THEM IN ORDER)	REASONS FOR YOUR RANKING
Safest:	
Least Safe:	

4. What conclusions about flood prevention can you think of as a result of answering 10 (a)?

_____

_____

THE VARIATION IN SEASONAL RUN-OFF

As precipitation varies from one season to another in various regions of Canada, so does the amount of run-off in the rivers.

1. Read question 11 (a) on page 187 in the textbook and record your answers below.

NAME OF RIVER AND REGION	SEASON(S) OF MAXIMUM FLOW	SEASON(S) OF MINIMUM FLOW	CLIMATIC REASONS FOR PATTERN OF FLOW

2. The river that appears to pose the greatest threat of flooding is the

_____ because _____

_____ .

p. 188

3. Answer question 12 on page 188 in the textbook.

    (a) The river that would be most difficult for ship transport is the

_____ because _____

_____

_____ .

    (b) The river that would be most suitable for ship transport would be the

_____ because _____

_____ .

GROUNDWATER

p.188

1.   **(a)** Groundwater is _____

_____ .

    (b) Pores are _____

_____ .

2. What importance does groundwater have for Canada's population? _____

_____

_____

3. On the following diagram, using Figure 6-8 on page 188 in the textbook as a guide, label the following items: groundwater and its movement (use arrows), river or lake, dry well, operating well, water table, and sand and gravel deposits.

GROUNDWATER AND THE WATER TABLE

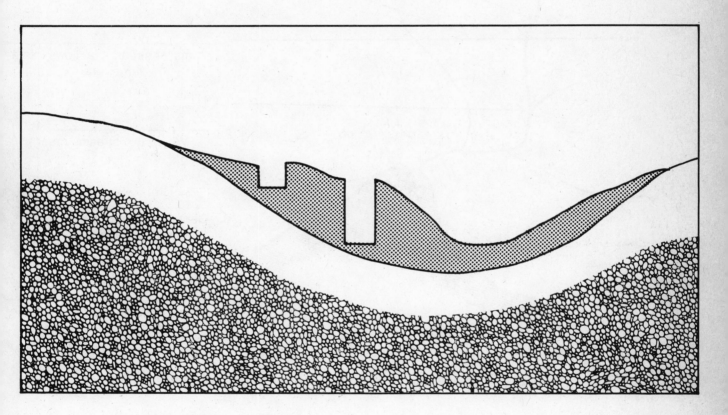

THE DRAINAGE BASIN OF A RIVER

1. Label this diagram of the drainage basin of a typical Canadian river. Figure 6-9 in the textbook will help you.

p. 189

① _____

Outside boundary of the drainage basin

② _____

Where a stream starts

③ _____

④ _____

Area inside the dotted line

⑤ _____

A smaller stream that flows into a larger one

⑥ _____

Where two streams meet

⑦ _____

General name for where a river flows out into a lake or the sea

⑧ _____

Where the end of a river is made up of soil or gravel islands

2. Explain the meaning of the following terms:

(a) Mouth _____

_____

(b) Tributary _____

_____

(c) Confluence _____

_____

(d) Watershed _____

3. Answer question 17 on page 189 in your textbook in the space provided below.

(a) _____

_____

(b) _____

_____

(c) _____

_____

_____

4. Using your atlas and Figure 6-10 on page 190 in the textbook, name the major drainage basins where each of the following settlements or features is located.

p. 190

SETTLEMENT	DRAINAGE BASIN
Yellowknife	_____
Corner Brook	_____
Sydney, N.S.	_____
Sept-Iles	_____
Mississauga	_____
Brandon	_____
Cypress Hills	_____ and _____
Prince George	_____
North Battleford	_____
Kitchener	_____
Moncton	_____
Thompson, Man.	_____

5. Many Canadian rivers flow to the north. What problems do you think this would present? Think especially about freeze-up time in the fall and spring thaw, and about temperature differences along a river.

_____

_____

_____

_____

6. Answer question 21 on page 190 in your textbook, using the chart below.

THUNDER BAY TO THE ATLANTIC OCEAN

	MAIN WATER USES	MAJOR AREAS FOR THE USE
(a)		
(b)		
(c)		
(d)		
(e)		
(f)		
(g)		
(h)		

WATER SURPLUS: PROBLEMS AND SOLUTIONS

p. 191

1. A water surplus occurs whenever _____

_____

_____ .

2. Some water surpluses are hardly noticed by the residents in an area. Other surpluses can be very serious in their impact. Give examples of what could cause each type.

Small water surplus   **(a)** _____

                                (b) _____

Serious water surplus (a) _____

(b) _____

3. The greatest amount of flooding occurs in Canada in the _____,

because _____ .

4. Have you ever seen flooding near your home? _____ If so, explain

where and when it occurred and how serious it was. _____

_____

_____

5. Answer question 22 at the bottom of page 191 of your textbook in the
space below. Refer to your atlas and Figure 6-12 on page 192.

pp. 191-192

(a) Major cities affected by spring flooding _____

_____

_____

(b) Rivers that flood good agricultural land _____

_____

_____

(c) The oceans to which flooding rivers eventually flow _____

_____

(d) Brief description of where in Canada the flooding frequently occurs

_____

_____

_____

6. Read question 25 on page 193 in your textbook, and then fill in this special report.

SPECIAL ASSIGNMENT SHEET

Occupation:	Newspaper Reporter
Home base:	Winnipeg Free Press
Special Assignment:	To report in detail about the flood damage in Carman, Manitoba
Transportation:	Helicopter to the site of flooding in Carman
Background brief:	Figure 6-13. The floodway is completely covered by water.

The report, to be filed before you leave, includes

(a) the buildings, roads, and facilities that have been flooded (half page)

_____

_____

_____

_____

_____

_____

_____

(b) the location and subjects for 15 photographs that you intend to take

_____

_____

_____

_____

(c) three types of people, each with different occupations, whom you intend to interview while you are in Carman

_____

_____

_____

_____

---

7. Why are cities on the Prairies, such as Winnipeg, particularly open to flood

damage? _____

_____

_____

8. Explain in your own words exactly how the Winnipeg Floodway would help

Winnipeg during a time of flooding. _____

_____

_____

WATER DEFICIT: PROBLEMS AND SOLUTIONS

1. How is a water deficit different from a drought? _____   *pp. 194-195*

_____

_____

2. Examine Figure 6-15 in the textbook, and then answer these questions.

   (a) Vancouver is shown to have a water deficit, and yet it receives a large
   amount of precipitation. Explain why it has a deficit at all. Consult
   Figure 2-43 on page 55 in the textbook for help.

   _____

   _____

   _____

   (b) The Arctic has no water deficit, and yet it receives little precipitation.
   Explain the reasons for this. (See Figure 2-43 on page 55 in the
   textbook.)

   _____

   _____

   _____

   (c) Which province has no water deficit? Explain why this is true. (See
   Figure 2-43 on page 55 in the textbook.)

   _____

   _____

   _____

3. Complete and label these two diagrams from Figure 6-16 of your textbook. Sketch in the lakes and water levels and any arrows.

During periods of heavy precipitation and run-off, this dam holds back water in an artificial lake. The people living at Z are pleased because

_____.

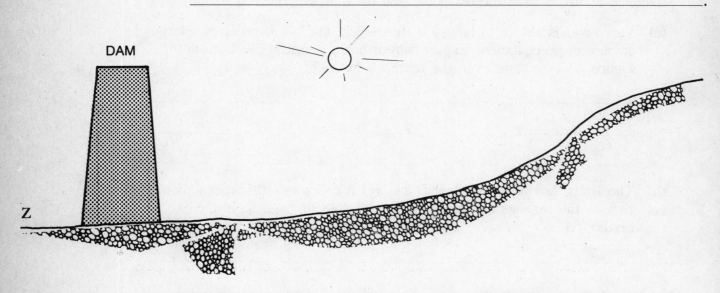

During a period of water deficit, water is slowly released from behind the dam. The people living at Z are pleased because _____

_____.

WATER MANAGEMENT

1. There is an increasing demand for water in Canada as our population grows and industry expands. In Ontario a number of conservation authorities have

been set up to _____

_____ .

Specific projects include _____ ,

_____ , _____ , and

_____ .

2. Using your atlas and Figure 6-17 in your textbook, name the cities that would benefit from the work of these conservation authorities in Ontario.

p. 197

CONSERVATION AUTHORITY   CITIES THAT BENEFIT

C.L.O. (Central Lake Ontario)   _____

Nottawasaga   _____

Essex   _____

Cataraqui   _____

Rideau   _____

Niagara   _____

Nickel District   _____

Lakehead   _____

MTRCA (Metropolitan Toronto
and Region)   _____

Grand   _____

Upper Thames   _____

3. **(a)** Design your own conservation authorities. On the accompanying map draw lines around each watershed or group of watersheds that could be managed as a unit. Use a red pencil or pen.

(b) Did you group any rivers together to form one conservation authority? _____ If so, explain why you did it. _____

_____

4. NAWAPA stands for _____ .

p. 198

The basic idea behind NAWAPA is to _____

_____ .

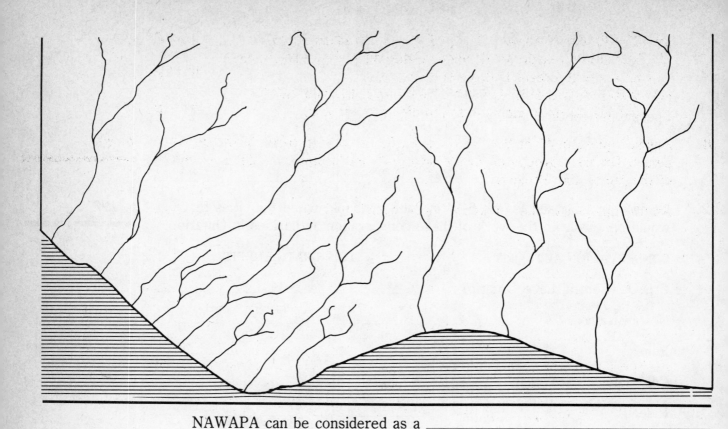

NAWAPA can be considered as a _____

program since resources would be transferred within _____

to wherever they are needed.

5.   Answer question 37 on page 199 of the textbook in the space below.

<table>
<tr><td colspan="2" align="center">ADVANTAGES</td><td colspan="2" align="center">DISADVANTAGES</td></tr>
<tr><td>(a)</td><td>_____</td><td>(a)</td><td>_____</td></tr>
<tr><td></td><td>_____</td><td></td><td>_____</td></tr>
<tr><td>(b)</td><td>_____</td><td>(b)</td><td>_____</td></tr>
<tr><td></td><td>_____</td><td></td><td>_____</td></tr>
<tr><td>(c)</td><td>_____</td><td>(c)</td><td>_____</td></tr>
<tr><td></td><td>_____</td><td></td><td>_____</td></tr>
</table>

6.   Nothing has actually been built in connection with NAWAPA. It is therefore

called a _____.

p. 199   7.   Answer T (True) or F (False) to each of the following questions about the
James Bay Project.

   (a) The James Bay Project is entirely within Quebec.   T   F
   (b) The original project was to affect approximately 20% of
Quebec's area.   T   F

(c) The first river to be developed was the Hudson River.   T   F

(d) The prime reason for developing the James Bay Project at first was to create hydro-electricity.   T   F

(e) Water from the St. Lawrence River was diverted into La Grande River to increase hydro-electric potential.   T   F

8. Answer question 41 at the top of page 201 of your textbook in the space below. Different groups of people have different attitudes to development of the James Bay Project.

p. 201

An unemployed worker in Quebec would think that _____

_____

_____

_____

_____.

A Cree Indian would think the project was a _____ idea because

_____

_____

_____

_____.

An American tourist would likely view the project as a _____

idea since _____

_____

_____

_____.

A manufacturer of heavy machinery in Quebec would be _____

the project because _____

_____

_____

_____.

An environmentalist would _____ the project because _____

_____

_____

_____.

POLLUTION

p. 201

1. Examine Figure 6-20 in the textbook and write a short paragraph, using full sentences, to describe the various sources of water pollution.

_____

_____

_____

_____

_____

_____

_____

_____

_____

_____

p. 202

2. Complete this diagram to help explain why acid rain occurs and how it damages the environment. Refer to Figure 6-22 on page 202 in your textbook.

THE PROBLEM OF ACID RAIN

3. The first problem in trying to solve acid rain is _____ _____

_____.

Once this is done, if it can be, there is the _____ _____

_____.

The solutions to both problems are very expensive.

4. **(a)** Using straight lines, join each stage in the left column with characteristics in the right column. *p. 203*

STAGE IN THE AGING OF LAKES	CHARACTERISTICS
	• Water is less clear, more plants
	• Clean water, few plants
Young •	• Lake is completely filled with debris
	• Cold water fish
Middle Age •	• Only a small river remains rather than a lake
	• Cold water, deep lake
Old Age •	• Shallowing lake
	• Build-up of debris on lake floor
	• Marshes are found where the lake once was

(b) What effect does water pollution have on the aging of lakes? _____

_____

5. Answer question 47 on page 203 in the textbook. *p. 203*

PLACE	CAUSE OF POLLUTION

6. Degradable pollution includes substances that _____

_____.

Examples include _____.

When discharged into lakes and rivers, degradable pollution robs _____

_____.

This is called _____.

7. Non-degradable pollution involves substances that _____

_____,

such as _____ and _____.

These may kill _____

_____.

8. What must Canadians do to ensure that their water resources are

preserved for the future?

_____

_____

_____

_____

VOCABULARY CROSSWORD

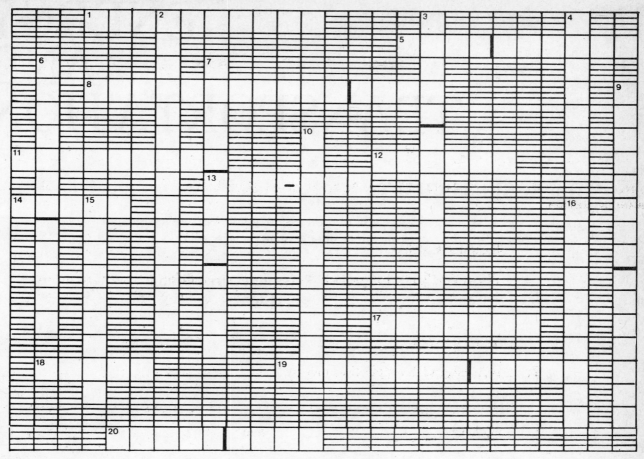

The answers are in the vocabulary on page 205 of the textbook and in Chapter 6.

CLUES

ACROSS

1. The top of the groundwater
5. The river into which tributaries flow (two words)
8. How water is recycled (two words)
11. The (high) land between one river system and the next
12. The beginning of a river
13. The water that flows off the surface of the land (one word, hyphenated)
14. The mouth of the Fraser River is a _____.
17. A long, dry spell
18. Holes in rock or soil
19. The land drained by one river and its tributaries (two words)
20. The likelihood of floods (two words)

DOWN

2. A process that uses up oxygen in lakes and rivers
3. Flooding results from a _____. (two words)
4. A water shortage is called a _____.
6. Water in rivers and lakes is called _____. (two words)
7. Maps that show the likelihood of flood damage (three words)
9. Plans for the development of natural materials (two words)
10. Water in the rocks and soil
15. A smaller stream or river that flows into a larger one
16. The point where two rivers meet

7

ENERGY AND TRANSPORTATION

PERSONAL PROGRESS CHART

Put a check mark in the first square for each section when your teacher assigns it. When you have completed the section, put a check mark in the second square.

Page	Topic	Assigned by teacher	Completed by you
181	Quiz	☐	☐
182	Present Energy Use	☐	☐
183	Renewable and Non-Renewable Energy	☐	☐
184	Oil	☐	☐
186	Offshore Drilling	☐	☐
187	Drilling in the Arctic	☐	☐
188	The Oil Sands	☐	☐
189	Electricity	☐	☐
189	Hydro-electricity	☐	☐
190	Thermal Electricity	☐	☐
190	Nuclear Electricity	☐	☐
191	Peak Periods of Demand	☐	☐
192	The North American Power Grid	☐	☐
192	Impact of Producing Electricity	☐	☐
192	Energy Alternatives: Active and Passive Solar Heating	☐	☐
195	Wind Power	☐	☐
195	Plant Material as Fuel	☐	☐

195   Tidal Power _____   ☐   ☐

196   Conservation _____   ☐   ☐

196   Transportation _____   ☐   ☐

200   Vocabulary Crossword _____   ☐   ☐

QUIZ

Answer this quiz by circling the most correct answer. The first ten questions are from page 208 of the textbook.   *p. 208*

1. If you had a chance, what would you buy?
   (a) a sports car
   (b) an 8-cylinder car with air conditioning
   (c) a compact 4-cylinder car
   (d) a van

2. On the highway, at what speed do you and your family normally drive?
   (a) 88-92 km/h
   (b) 70-87 km/h
   (c) more than 92 km/h

3. Have you discussed the rising cost of energy in your home in the last six months?
   (a) yes   **(b)** no

4. When you wash, do you normally
   (a) shower?   **(b)** bathe?

5. Does the washing machine that cleans your clothes recycle wash water for a second load?
   (a) yes   **(b)** no   **(c)** do not know

6. To get a drink of water, do you let the water run to get cold?
   (a) yes   **(b)** no

7. When you leave a room for more than five minutes, do you ordinarily leave the lights on?
   (a) yes   **(b)** no

8. Which of the following appliances does your household regularly use?
   (a) electric can opener
   (b) garage heater
   (c) blow dryer for your hair
   (d) flood lights

9. What temperature is your home generally kept at during the winter?
   (a) 20°C   **(b)** under 20°C   **(c)** over 20°C

10. Evaluate this statement as true or false.
    Since you are only one person, you cannot really do anything to help cut down energy use in Canada.

Once you have completed questions 1 to 10, turn to page 237 in the textbook for

your energy rating. What was your score? _____

What comment was written about your score? _____

Now continue the quiz.

11. Which gives more light?
    (a) a 40-W incandescent light bulb
    (b) a 40-W fluorescent tube
12. The least power-hungry oven is the
    (a) conventional oven
    (b) self-cleaning oven
    (c) continuous-clean oven.
13. If you never opened the refrigerator door, how much energy would you save of the total required to operate it?
    (a) a quarter
    (b) a third
    (c) a half
14. Which type of freezer is the most energy-efficient?
    (a) upright
    (b) chest
15. How much of the heat from a conventional oven actually goes to cooking the food?
    (a) 12%   (b) 35%   (c) 64%
16. Dishwashers use
    (a) more water than hand washing
    (b) less water than hand washing
    (c) about the same amount of water as hand washing.
17. Which of these takes the most electricity, on the average?
    (a) refrigeration
    (b) cooking
    (c) lighting
18. If your refrigerator cost $600 to buy, how much would it cost to run for 10 years?
    (a) $120   (b) $300   (c) $600
19. It is most economical to bake a pie in a
    (a) glass dish
    (b) disposable foil plate
    (c) standard aluminum pie plate.
20. How much energy would you save by boiling water in an electric kettle instead of on top of the stove?
    (a) 10%   (b) 15%   (c) 20%

For answers, turn to the end of this chapter and see what your score is.

PRESENT ENERGY USE

pp. 208-209

1. Look at Figure 7-1 and describe how energy use has changed. _____

_____

_____

2. Explain why we use much more energy than our ancestors. _____

_____

_____

3. Plot the information from the chart about sources of energy, found on page 209 of the textbook, on the bar graph that follows.

CANADA'S SOURCES OF ENERGY

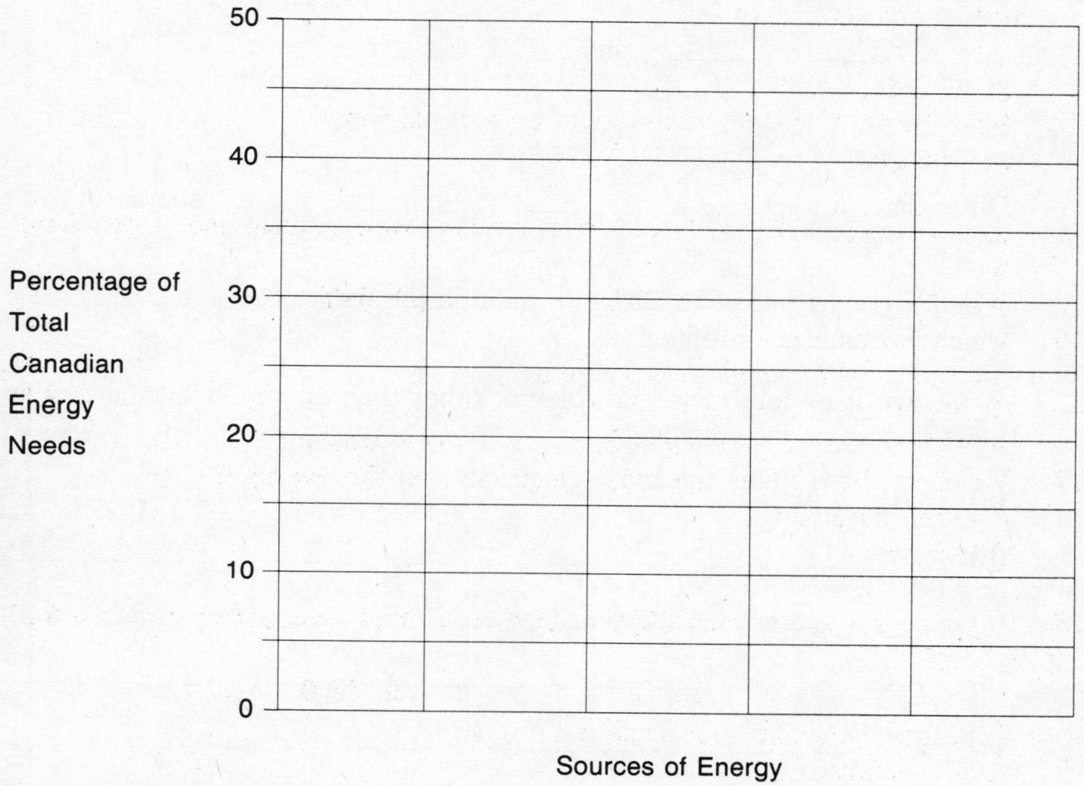

Percentage of
Total
Canadian
Energy
Needs

50

40

30

20

10

0

Sources of Energy

Energy Efficiency

1. Answer question 5 below Figure 7-2 on page 210 of the textbook. *p. 210*

(a) _____ (%),   **(e)** _____ (%),
(highest efficiency)   (percentage of
energy wasted)

(b) _____ (%),   **(f)** _____ (%),

(c) _____ (%),   **(g)** _____ (%).

(d) _____ (%),

RENEWABLE AND NON-RENEWABLE ENERGY

1. **(a)** Outline the meaning of non-renewable energy. _____ *p. 210*

_____

(b) Three examples are _____ , _____ ,

and _____ .

2. **(a)** What does renewable energy mean? _____

_____

_____

(b) Give three examples of renewable energy: _____ ,

_____ , and _____ .

OIL

p. 211

1. Oil is Canada's _____ _____ source of
energy today.

2. When it comes out of the ground, oil is in the form of _____ ,
which is crude or unrefined oil.

3. Write five uses for refined petroleum, other than energy, that you feel are
most important for your life.

(a) _____

(b) _____

(c) _____

(d) _____

(e) _____

4. Using Figure 7-4 in your textbook as a guide, label the diagram below.
Give it a suitable title.

TITLE: _____

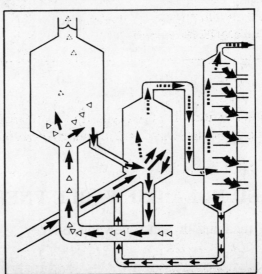

5.   **(a)** What is distillation? _____

_____

(b) What is cracking? _____

_____

6.   **(a)** On the following map of Canada, mark the oil and gas fields (present
and potential) as well as the pipelines.
(Use an X to mark your home.)
Use the key to show the meanings of the colours and symbols that
you have used on the map.

p. 212

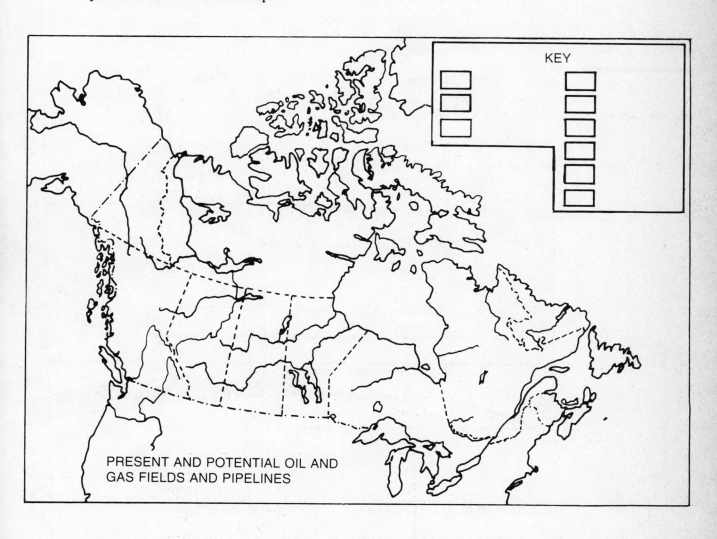

KEY

PRESENT AND POTENTIAL OIL AND
GAS FIELDS AND PIPELINES

(b) Describe the location of oil and gas deposits relative to your home.
Are they close or far away, and in which direction do they lie?

_____

_____

_____

7. Oil has been called "black gold" because _____

_____

_____ .

8. Most oil is not found oozing to the surface of the earth. It is usually buried

deep in the earth. Petroleum can be discovered using

_____ , _____ , and

_____ . A common type of equipment used is the

_____ .

p. 214

9. Fully label this diagram.

How Oil and Natural Gas May Be Trapped in
Rocks beneath the Surface

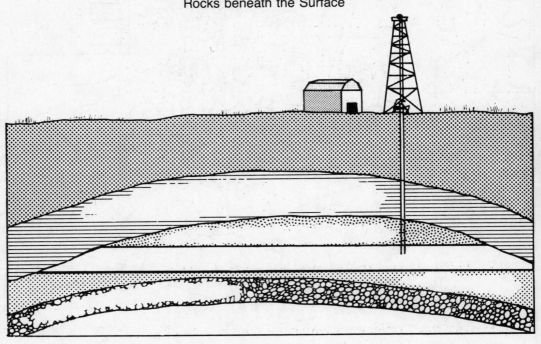

OFFSHORE DRILLING

p. 214

1. Some oil is found on our continental shelf, which is a _____

_____ .

Searching for oil on the continental shelf is called _____ .

2. (a) Label this diagram of an offshore drilling rig.

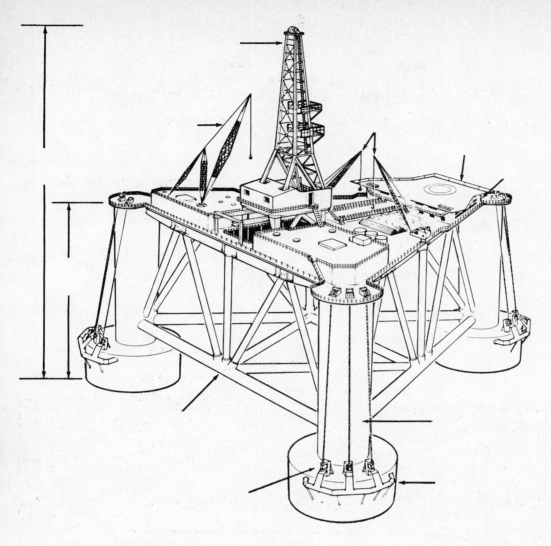

(b) Why are these drilling rigs like floating islands? _____ *p. 215*

_____

(c) Why must drilling crews be extremely careful? _____

_____

_____

DRILLING IN THE ARCTIC

1. Write five lines, using your own words, to describe the various problems associated with drilling in the Arctic. *p. 215*

_____

_____

_____

p. 216
2. Examine Figure 7-10 in your textbook. Briefly describe the opinion that each of the following people would have of the Arctic pipeline.

(a) A typical motorist in Toronto _____

_____

_____

(b) An unemployed worker in the Northwest Territories _____

_____

_____

(c) An environmentalist _____

_____

_____

(d) An Inuit living in the Arctic _____

_____

_____

(e) A steelworker making pipes in Hamilton _____

_____

_____

p. 218
3. Examine Figure 7-12 on page 218 in the textbook and briefly describe Canada's present oil situation.

_____

_____

_____

THE OIL SANDS

p. 218
1. (a) What are the oil sands? _____

_____

(b) In what part of which province are they mainly located?

_____

2. Explain why the oil sands projects are so expensive.

_____

_____

_____

_____

3. What is a boom town? _____ _p. 219_

_____

4. What do you think would cause a boom town to go "bust," with people

losing their jobs and many leaving the area? _____

_____

_____

ELECTRICITY

1. Explain the meaning of megajoule (MJ). _____ _p. 220_

_____

2. Complete this chart.

THE COST OF VARIOUS ELECTRICAL APPLIANCES

ELECTRICAL DEVICE	AVERAGE USE OF ENERGY PER YEAR (MJ)	COST PER MEGAJOULE (1985)	TOTAL COST PER YEAR ($)
Clock	61.2 ×	1.17¢ =	$0.72
Clothes Dryer	4320 ×	1.17¢ =	
Frying Pan	864 ×	1.17¢ =	
Hair Dryer	54 ×	1.17¢ =	
Stove Range	5580 ×	1.17¢ =	
Shaver	2.16 ×	1.17¢ =	
Colour Television	1944 ×	1.17¢ =	
Toaster	180 ×	1.17¢ =	
Vacuum Cleaner	162 ×	1.17¢ =	
Light Bulbs	6732 ×	1.17¢ =	

NOTE: The expression MJ means megajoule. The figures in the table are Canadian averages; regional variations will alter them somewhat.

HYDRO-ELECTRICITY

1. Hydro-electricity is produced _____ and _p. 221_

now provides _____ % of our electrical needs.

p. 223

2. Label this diagram to explain how water produces electricity.

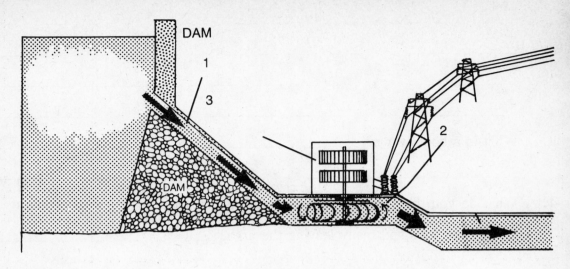

THERMAL ELECTRICITY

p. 223

1. With thermal electricity, _____ rather than _____ turns the turbine to produce electrical power.

2. Complete and label this diagram of a thermal power plant.

A THERMAL POWER PLANT

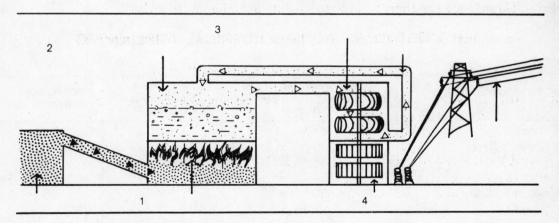

NUCLEAR ELECTRICITY

p. 223

1. The heat that produces steam for the turbines in a nuclear power plant comes from a _____.

2. Sketch and label your own diagram to illustrate a nuclear reaction. Use Figure 7-21 to help you.

3. In Canada, nuclear electricity is produced in a _____ .

    A major concern about nuclear electricity is the possibility of escape of

    _____ . This can hurt or even kill people.

PEAK PERIODS OF DEMAND

1. The unique character of electricity means that it must be _____ *p. 224*

    as soon as it is produced. This presents quite a problem since electricity

    cannot be _____ on any large scale.

2. **(a)** Generally, the peak electricity use during the year is from

    _____ to _____ .

    (b) Answer question 29 on page 224 in your textbook.

    _____

    _____

3. List four reasons why demand for electricity varies so much through the
    day. (See Figure 7-23 in the textbook.)

    (a) _____

    (b) _____

    (c) _____

    (d) _____

THE NORTH AMERICAN POWER GRID

p. 225

1. **(a)** What is a power grid? _____

_____

(b) Explain the usefulness of the power grid. _____

_____

_____

IMPACT OF PRODUCING ELECTRICITY

p. 226

Examine Figure 7-25 on page 226 of the textbook. Write ten lines to compare natural gas and coal as energy sources for producing electricity. Include as many similarities and differences as you can discover.

_____

_____

_____

_____

_____

_____

_____

_____

_____

_____

ENERGY ALTERNATIVES: ACTIVE AND PASSIVE SOLAR HEATING

p. 227

1. In the space provided, draw and fully label a diagram to illustrate active solar heating in a house. Examine Figure 7-26 in the textbook before you draw your diagram.

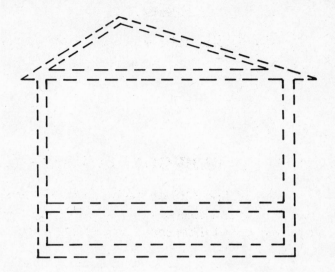

2. The first apartment building in Canada to be heated entirely by solar

energy was opened in the summer of _____ near

_____ , Ontario. Active solar heating is

_____ to install but relatively _____

to run.

3. Devices have been developed that convert solar energy to electricity. They

are called _____ .

4. One experimental house in Prince Edward Island, called _____ ,

was designed to be heated with _____ . It has been

abandoned because of the cost of running it.

5. Passive solar heating involves _____ *p. 228*

_____ .

6. Answer questions 41 to 46 from page 228 of your textbook in the space
provided below.

Your Advertisement

WIND POWER

Although wind is _____ , it does not blow _____ .   *p. 229*

Wind power is suitable for only some regions of Canada, such as the

_____ or the _____ . For the rest of

Canada, windmills could only be _____ .

PLANT MATERIAL AS FUEL

1. What is biomass conversion? _____   *p. 229*

    _____

2. Explain how trees could be used for energy. _____

    _____

    _____

    _____

TIDAL POWER

1. Tides are _____   *p. 230*

    _____ .

2. Complete the following diagrams and explain how to use tidal power to generate electricity.

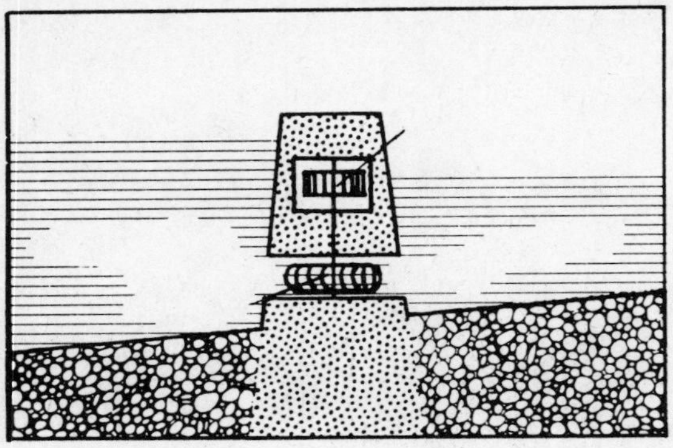

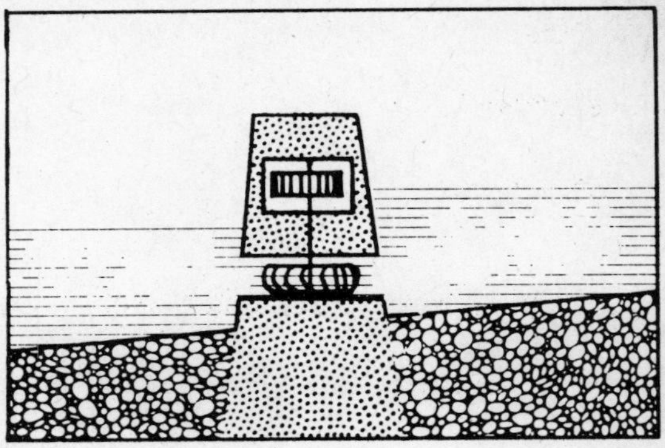

_____   _____

_____   _____

_____   _____

_____   _____

_____   _____

CONSERVATION

p. 231

Explain in your own words the importance of conservation to Canada's future.

_____

_____

_____

_____

_____

TRANSPORTATION

p. 231

1. Which two aspects of Canada's geography make a transportation network so important?

   (a) _____

   (b) _____

p. 234

2. Answer question 57 on page 234 of your textbook using this chart.

COMMODITY	SPECIAL CONDITIONS FOR THE TRANSPORTATION OF COMMODITIES	TYPES OF TRANSPORTATION POSSIBLE (EXAMPLE: REFRIGERATED TRUCK)
Eggs		
People		
Ice cream		
Gasoline		

3. Most of the Canadian Arctic is so isolated that no _____ or

_____ comes close. Since the Arctic Ocean is _____

or _____ most of the year, ship transportation is very

difficult. Weather conditions are often _____.

_____ , _____ , and _____

can suddenly develop, making aircraft travel dangerous or impossible.

4. There are two major highways built into the Canadian North or Arctic.

These are the _____ and the _____ .

Resources such as _____ and _____ can

reach the markets via one of these highways.

5. What is a grid pattern? _____

_____

6. Following Figure 7-35 in your textbook, construct a grid pattern of
streets. Use the road drawn here to begin your street pattern.

p. 235

pp. 232-235

7. Most transportation routes in Canada are in the _____ .
(north/south)
In addition, _____ % of all transportation activity in our country takes

place in _____ areas such as Edmonton.

p. 236

8. An Area for Resource Development

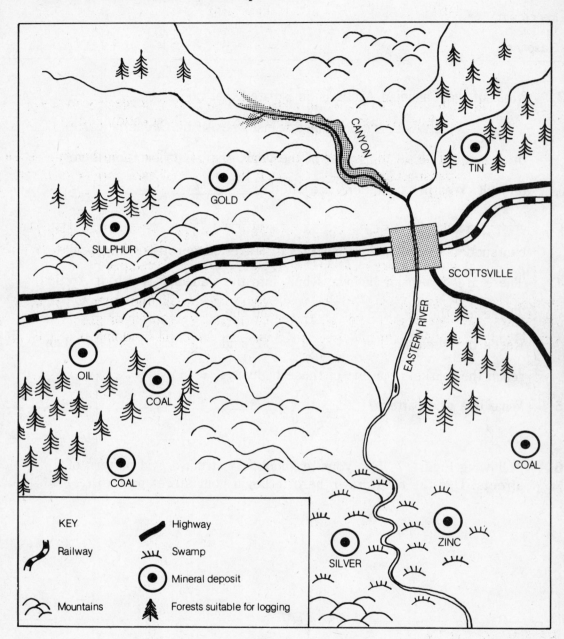

Answer question 62 on page 236 of the textbook in the space below.

(62) **(a)** The three resources that should be developed first are

(i) _____ because _____

_____

_____ .

(ii) _____ because _____

_____

_____ .

(iii) _____ because _____

_____

_____ .

(b) On the map, mark the transportation routes necessary to bring out the resources you chose to develop in question 62(a).

Circle on the map the problems that would be faced building these transportation routes. Explain the nature of each problem on the map.

(c) Which three resources do you feel are not worth developing at present? Put an X through each of these. Beside each one, write an explanation of why they should not be developed.

In this space, draw a picture of what you would like to see the transportation of the future look like. (You could design public transportation, air or space vehicles, for example.) Do not draw a private car. You will be doing this later on.

ENERGY QUIZ

Answers to questions 11 through 20.
11: (b) 12: (b) 13: (b) 14: (a) 15: (a) 17: (a) 16: (b) 18: (c) 19: (a)
20: (c)

If you scored 7 to 10, you know quite a bit about conservation. Good. If you scored 5 or 6, you have some knowledge of energy saving. If you scored below 5, you need to learn much more.

VOCABULARY CROSSWORD

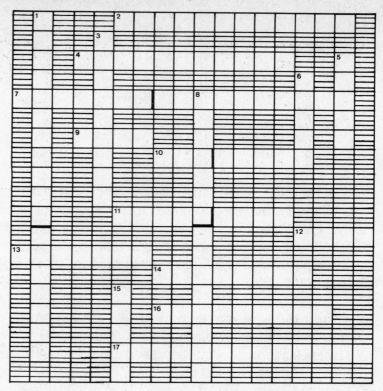

The answers are in the textbook on page 237 and in Chapter 7.

Clues

ACROSS

2. A process involving evaporation and condensation
4. An instrument that records vibrations in the ground
7. Using plant material to create other forms of energy (two words)
9. A _____ town is one that has grown very quickly.
10. These are located near Fort McMurray. (two words)
11. The electrical lines that transport electricity across Canada (two words)
12. A pattern of lines that cross each other, normally at right angles
13. Coal is used to produce _____ power.
14. A stage in the refining of oil
16. The most commonly used fuel for cars
17. Dangerous rays from a nuclear reaction

DOWN

1. The extensions of the continents beneath shallow seas (two words)
3. MJ
5. The Canadian type of nuclear reactor
6. The twice-daily fluctuations of the ocean level
8. A _____ releases energy by splitting atoms. (two words)
15. Power produced from falling water is called _____ -electric power.

OUR NATURAL RESOURCES AND HOW WE USE THEM

8

PERSONAL PROGRESS CHART

Put a check mark in the first square for each section when your teacher assigns it. When you have completed the section, put a check mark in the second square.

Page	Topic	Assigned by teacher	Completed by you
202	Natural Resources	☐	☐
204	Mining	☐	☐
204	The Importance of Mining to Canada	☐	☐
205	The Distribution of Mining in Canada	☐	☐
206	Locating Valuable Deposits	☐	☐
206	Developing a Mine	☐	☐
209	Potash in Saskatchewan	☐	☐
211	The Importance of Canadian Mining Products to the U.S.A.	☐	☐
211	Some Problems Associated with Mining	☐	☐
212	The Mining Game	☐	☐
212	Forestry	☐	☐
214	The Importance of Canadian Forests	☐	☐
214	Forest Inventory	☐	☐
216	Modern Methods of Forest Management	☐	☐
216	Transporting the Timber to the Mill	☐	☐

217	Forest Fires _____	☐	☐
218	The Pulp and Paper Industry _____	☐	☐
221	Environmental Problems Associated with the Forestry Industry _____	☐	☐
223	The Fishing Industry _____	☐	☐
224	Fishing off the Coast of the Atlantic Provinces _____	☐	☐
226	Fishing Methods and Fish Caught _____	☐	☐
228	Shellfish _____	☐	☐
228	The Pacific Coast Fisheries _____	☐	☐
230	Inland Fisheries _____	☐	☐
230	Protecting Our Fisheries _____	☐	☐
232	Vocabulary Crossword _____	☐	☐

NATURAL RESOURCES

p. 239

1. Natural objects become resources when we learn to _____.

2. From this list, circle those objects that you think could be or might become natural resources. Beside every item, explain why it is or is not a natural resource.

   Oil deposit _____

   _____

   A school building _____

   _____

   A rocky island in a lake _____

   _____

   Beavers _____

   _____

3. From Figure 8-1 on page 239 in the textbook, list the types of objects that are normally classed as natural resources.

   _____   _____   _____

   _____   _____   _____

4. **(a)** _____ resources are those that can replace themselves once they are used.

(b) _____ resources cannot replace themselves. Once they are used up, they are said to be _____.

5. Below is a list of eight objects. Beside each one write R for renewable or NR for non-renewable.
    - fish
    - Niagara Falls
    - frogs
    - mosquitoes
    - the Canadian Shield
    - forests
    - moose
    - metals

6. **(a)** Explain why water is considered to be a renewable resource. _____

    _____

    _____

    (b) What might cause water to become exhausted? _____

    _____

7. **(a)** Explain three ways in which natural resources were important in the development of Canada in the past.

    (i) _____

    (ii) _____

    (iii) _____

    (b) How would the exploitation (use) of a resource in a remote part of Canada lead to further development of the country? Name three ways.

    (i) _____

    (ii) _____

    (iii) _____

8. Answer questions 4, 5, and 6 at the bottom of page 240 in the textbook. _p. 240_

    (4) I can tell that Thompson is a planned town because _____

    _____.

    (5) I think that there are no very tall buildings in Thompson because _____

    _____.

(6) **(a)** Before the town, mine, and smelter were started at Thompson,

_____

_____

_____.

(b) To attract workers to a remote centre like Thompson, a mining

company would _____

_____

_____

_____.

MINING

Choose any room, like your classroom, living room, or bedroom, and look around it carefully. Name ten objects that come from minerals.

_____ _____ _____ _____ _____

_____ _____ _____ _____ _____

THE IMPORTANCE OF MINING TO CANADA

p. 241

1. Mining makes up _____ percent of the total value of our

   exports. It also creates much _____. Mining also supports

   many other _____.

2. Look at Figure 8-6 on page 242 of the textbook. There are 12 adults and one child in the photograph. These are the adults' jobs: computer technician, laboratory chemist, miner, rock scientist, nurse, economist, day-care worker, secretary, truck driver, two laboratory assistants, college student with summer job. Match the correct job with each person on the diagram below.

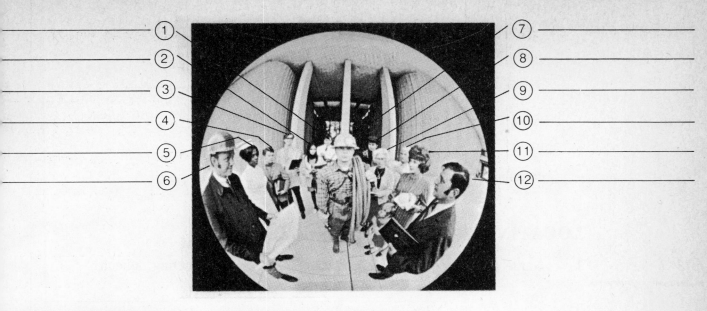

THE DISTRIBUTION OF MINING IN CANADA

1. Look at Figure 8-7 on page 242 of your textbook, and answer these questions.

p. 242

   (a) Which two provinces have most of our iron ore? _____

     _____

   (b) Where would you find most of our oil and gas? _____

   (c) Which mineral is very important in Saskatchewan? _____

   (d) Which province is first in the production of five minerals?

     _____

   (e) Which three provinces are first in three minerals?

     _____ _____ _____

   (f) The Northwest Territories are huge, and yet they do not produce many minerals. Suggest two reasons for this.

     (i) _____

     (ii) _____

2. In the folded mountain areas of the west and east, the minerals consist

mainly of _____ and _____, such as

_____, _____,

_____, and _____. In the fairly flat

areas of the Interior Plains and the Great Lakes–St. Lawrence Lowlands,

_____, _____, and

_____ minerals, such as _____

_____, and _____, are being

mined. The _____ _____

contains mainly metallic deposits.

LOCATING VALUABLE DEPOSITS

p. 243 1. Name four kinds of problems that made early prospecting difficult.

    (a) _____ **(c)** _____

    (b) _____ **(d)** _____

2. What kinds of equipment did the early prospectors use?

_____

3. Prospecting today is very different. Read "Locating Valuable Deposits" on pages 243 to 244 of the textbook and look at the six photographs showing modern techniques on page 243.

    (a) Describe what kinds of equipment are involved in locating valuable deposits.

_____

_____

_____

    (b) Name four kinds of skills that prospectors would need in the activities described or shown on page 243 in your textbook.

        (i) _____ **(iii)** _____

        (ii) _____ **(iv)** _____

p. 244 4. An ore is _____.

DEVELOPING A MINE

1. List the six steps involved in developing a mine. (They are included in the first paragraph of this section on page 244 in the textbook.)

    (a) _____

    (b) _____

(c) _____

(d) _____

(e) _____

(f) _____

2. The two major methods of mining an ore are called _____

or _____ pit mining and _____ or

_____ mining.

3. Open pit mining is used when a deposit is close to the _____.

First the _____ or covering of rock and soil is scraped or

blasted away and then the _____ is exposed.

4.

② _____   ⑥ _____

③ _____   ⑦ _____

① _____   ④ _____

④ _____   ⑤ _____

The above sketch is based on Figure 8-11 on page 244 in your textbook.
In this limestone quarry there are many activities going on. Think carefully
and label the diagram as well as you can to show the activities and the
parts of the mine.

5. **(a)** Underground mining is used when the deposit is _____ in the   *p. 245*

_____.

(b) It is more _____ and _____ than
open pit mining.

6. Label the diagram of an underground mine, using Figure 8-14 on page 245 of the textbook as a guide. Include explanations of as many activities as you can.

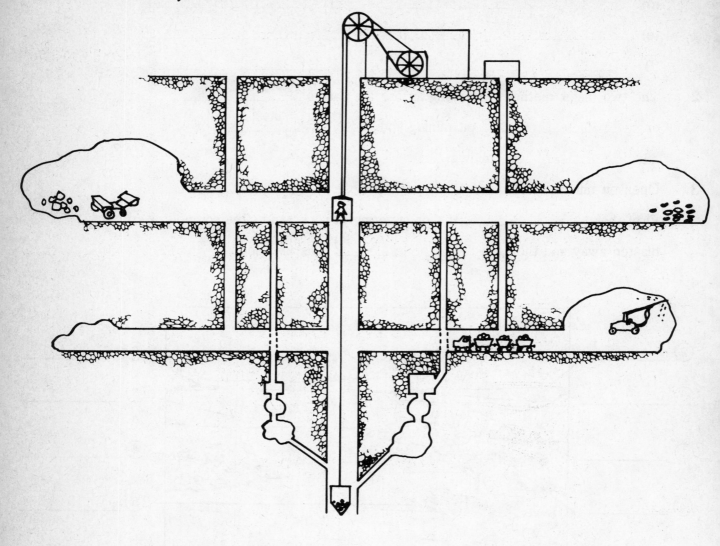

7. Describe how loosened ore gets from the stope to the surface.

_____

_____

_____

_____

_____

8. Give two reasons why underground mining is more dangerous than surface mining.

(a) _____

_____

(b) _____

_____

9. A mill is usually close to the mine. Describe what occurs in the mill, and why it is done.

p. 246

_____

_____

_____

_____

_____

10. Pictured below is the mine shown in Figure 8-13 on page 245 of the textbook. Use arrows and labels to identify as many of the features listed as you can.

p. 245

- mine buildings
- mill
- rail line
- road
- houses
- water tower
- arena
- pile of ore

POTASH IN SASKATCHEWAN

1. The main use for potash is as an ingredient in _____.

p. 246

Canada is a major _____ _____ of

_____. The major producing province is

_____. Most of our potash is _____

to other countries.

2. How did potash form originally? _____

p. 248

_____

_____

_____

3. Name the two ways of mining potash.

   (a) _____

   (b) _____

p. 249

4. Finish and label the following diagram, using Figure 8-22 on page 249 of the textbook as a guide.

SOLUTION MINING OF POTASH

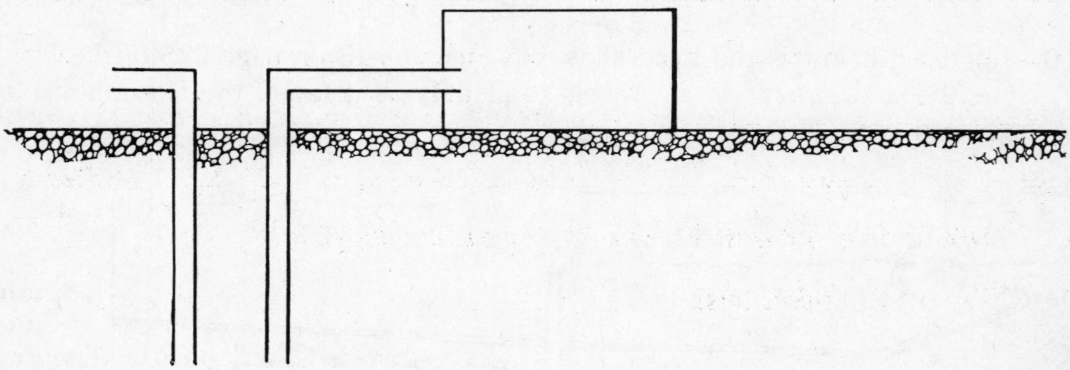

5. (a) What happened to prices when too much potash was produced in the early 1960s? _____

   _____

   (b) What happened as a result of this? _____

   _____

6. What two policies did the government introduce to help stabilize potash production? Explain each.

   (a) _____

   _____

   (b) _____

   _____

7. What are royalties? _____

   _____

THE IMPORTANCE OF CANADIAN MINING PRODUCTS TO THE U.S.A.

1. Read the short paragraph at the bottom of page 249 in the textbook. List the advantages and disadvantages of selling our minerals abroad.

p. 249

ADVANTAGES	DISADVANTAGES

2. What is your opinion? Should we export our minerals? _____

   Why do you think this? _____

   _____

SOME PROBLEMS ASSOCIATED WITH MINING

1. Fill in the diagram below, based on Figure 8-23 from page 250 of the textbook.

p. 250

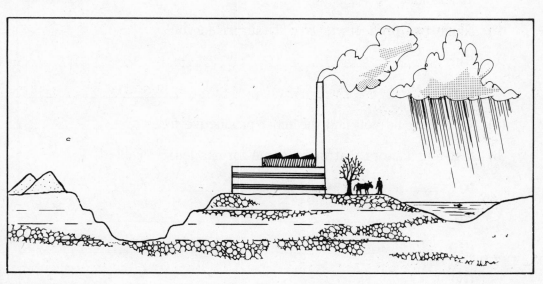

_____ can be controlled, but the processes are

_____.

p. 251

2. Nobody likes to live in a polluted environment. Write down three reasons why many industries, including mining, continue to pollute.

(a) _____

(b) _____

(c) _____

THE MINING GAME

Play in groups of two, three, or four. You will need a marker for each person and a die for the group. Everyone puts markers on START; the first to reach FINISH is the winner. Throw the die to start; the highest goes first. ——————→

FORESTRY

p. 251

1. What percentage of Canada is covered by forests? _____

SOME PRODUCTS DERIVED FROM
A TREE

p. 252

2. **(a)** Draw your own tree in in space on the right. Mark on your tree ten products you are familiar with that come from trees. Use Figure 8-26 on page 252 of your textbook as a guide.

(b) Name two products that really surprised you!

(i) _____

(ii) _____

3. **(a)** Where would you find the most productive forests? _____

(b) List four factors that make some forests less valuable.

(i) _____

(ii) _____

(iii) _____

(iv) _____

START

NO MAPS EXIST, miss a turn

GOOD MAPS OF AREA, take an extra turn

GEOPHYSICAL STUDIES SHOW PROMISE, move forward 2

AIRCRAFT CRASHES, miss a turn

DEPOSIT POOR, go back to START

DEPOSIT LARGE AND RICH, go forward 4 spaces

GEOLOGISTS FIND POSSIBLE DEPOSIT, go forward 2

WEATHER BAD, miss a turn

RAISE CAPITAL EASILY, go forward 2

BUILD RAIL CONNECTION, go forward 2

CONSTRUCTION WORKERS STRIKE, go back 2

WORKERS GET LARGE PAY RAISE, go back 1

PROFITS HIGH, go forward 2

WORLD MARKET SAGS, miss a turn

ROYALTIES INCREASED Go back 2

MINE EXHAUSTED Go back 2

EXPORTS INCREASE Go forward 3

FINISH

THE IMPORTANCE OF CANADIAN FORESTS

p. 252

Fill in the blanks.

Canada contains about _____% of the productive forests of the world.

_____ and _____ is Canada's largest manufacturing

industry. We export _____, _____, and

other _____ products to over _____ countries. This

makes up _____ % of our total export earnings.

    Nearly _____ people are employed in the forestry and forestry

_____ industries. Indirectly _____ of

_____ of additional people are employed. For example, pulp and

paper mills use _____ of all the electrical power consumed in

Canada. Also every _____ freight car on our railways contains

_____ or _____ products.

FOREST INVENTORY

p. 252

1. What is a forest inventory? _____
2. Describe the three methods used in a forest inventory.

 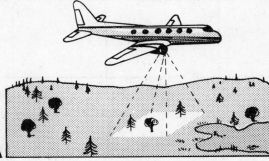 

3. Look at Figure 8-28 on page 253 of the textbook. *p. 253*

    (a) Which province has the most timber? _____ What

    kind is most of the timber in that province? _____

    (b) Which two other provinces are important producers?

    _____ and _____

    (c) List, in descending order, the three provinces that produce most hardwoods.

    _____ _____ _____
    (most)

    (d) Why do the Yukon and Northwest Territories produce little timber?

    _____

4. Fill in this diagram, based on the sketch at the bottom of page 253 in your textbook.

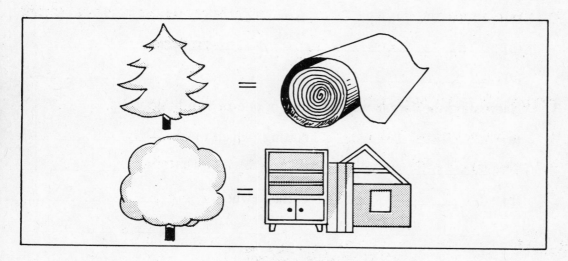

5. Below is a list of ten wood products. Divide them into two groups, those made from hardwoods and those made from softwoods.
- ice hockey sticks, toilet paper, matchsticks, cedar decking, maple table, salad bowl, house frames, playing cards, slow-burning firewood, an expensive wood carving

SOFTWOODS	HARDWOODS
(a) _____	**(a)** _____
(b) _____	**(b)** _____
(c) _____	**(c)** _____
(d) _____	**(d)** _____
(e) _____	**(e)** _____

MODERN METHODS OF FOREST MANAGEMENT

p. 254

1. In what ways are our forests

   (a) a home for wildlife _____

   _____

   (b) important in ensuring a year-round supply of water _____

   _____

   (c) areas for recreation _____

   _____

   (d) important in preventing soil erosion _____

   _____

2. What three important activities are involved in good forest management?

   (a) _____

   (b) _____

   (c) _____

3. Harvesting the forest may be done in one of two basic ways.

   (a) _____ cutting, which means _____

   _____

   (b) _____ cutting, when _____

   _____

TRANSPORTING THE TIMBER TO THE MILL

p. 257

Using Figure 8-36 on page 257 of the textbook as a guide, draw a flow chart that shows how timber gets from the tree to the mill.

216 Across Canada Second Edition: Student Workbook

Copyright © 1987 John Wiley & Sons Canada Limited

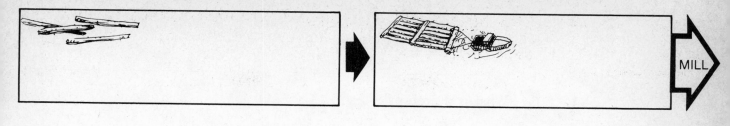

MILL

FOREST FIRES

Read the section and look at the photographs on pages 257 to 258 in your textbook. Answer the following questions.

1. List five causes of forest fires. In each case state whether the fire is due to carelessness, accident, or natural causes. Four are listed in the text; think of one additional cause.

    (a) _____

    (b) _____

    (c) _____

    (d) _____

    (e) _____

2. Explain two ways in which you can help prevent forest fires when in a forested area.

    (a) _____

    _____

    (b) _____

    _____

3. List and briefly describe five methods used to *prevent* forest fires from breaking out. *pp. 258-259*

    (a) _____

    _____

    (b) _____

    _____

    (c) _____

    _____

    (d) _____

    _____

(e) _____

_____

4. **(a)** What is a firebreak? _____

_____

(b) How does a firebreak help to prevent fires from spreading through the forest?

_____

_____

5. List three methods used to *fight* forest fires.

(a) _____

(b) _____

(c) _____

6. Lives are often lost trying to control forest fires. Why is this kind of fire fighting so dangerous? Think of three specific examples of how lives could be lost in forest fire fighting.

(a) _____

(b) _____

(c) _____

THE PULP AND PAPER INDUSTRY

p. 259

1. Fill in the blanks.

Pulp and paper is Canada's _____ _____

industry. Its products make up _____% of our exports and are valued

at over $_____ annually. Canada contains _____% of the

world's productive forests. The forestry industry directly employs

_____ people.

2. Make a list of ten different types of paper products that you use. Describe the characteristics of the paper in each product. These characteristics could be the feel, colour, strength, or purpose of the paper.

(a) _____

(b) _____

(c) _____

(d) _____

(e) _____

(f) _____

(g) _____

(h) _____

(i) _____

(j) _____

3. Complete the diagram below by fully labelling it. Refer to Figure 8-43 on page 260 of the textbook.

_p. 260_

THE REQUIREMENTS FOR A PULP AND PAPER MILL

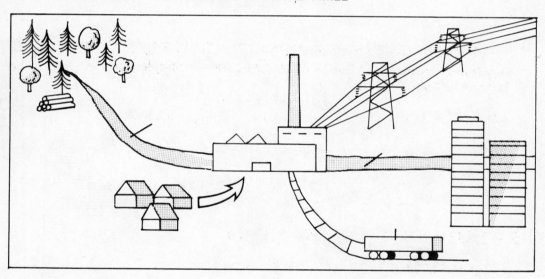

4. Look at Figure 8-44 on page 260 of the textbook. The sentences below describe the process of paper making, but they are in the wrong order. Carefully number the order in which they should have been written, and then write them out in the correct order.

The logs are sprayed with water.
The chipped and ground woods are mixed with water and chemicals.
The mixture goes through the paper machine where it dries into a thin layer.
The bark is removed from the logs.
The paper is made into huge rolls.
Some of the wood goes through a chipper, the rest through a grinder.

HOW PAPER IS MADE

_____
_____
_____
_____
_____
_____
_____
_____

p. 261

5. List the three provinces that produce most of our pulp and paper.

_____ _____ _____
(most)

6. Answer question 35 on page 262 of the textbook. Part 35 (a) is done for you. Use this map to answer parts (b), (c), and (d).

TITLE: _____

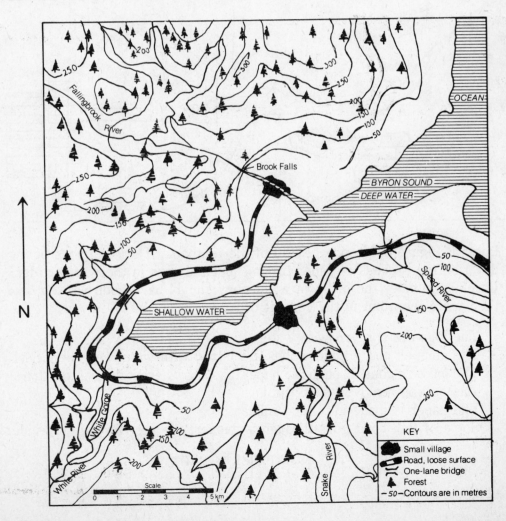

(35) **(e)** Write an account to accompany your map. It should be in the form of a report to the directors of the Pulp and Paper Industry and should carefully explain

(i) the advantages of the sites you have suggested for each mill and

(ii) the reasons for the other developments.

_____

_____

_____

_____

_____

_____

_____

_____

_____

_____

_____

_____

_____

_____

_____

_____

_____

ENVIRONMENTAL PROBLEMS ASSOCIATED WITH THE FORESTRY INDUSTRY

1. Fill in the following table, using Figure 8-48 on page 263 of the textbook.

_p. 263_

PROBLEMS ASSOCIATED WITH THE FORESTRY INDUSTRY

CAUSE OF POLLUTION	RESULTS FROM POLLUTION	ADDITIONAL COMMENTS
Spraying	Dangerous to human and animal life	Important in insect control. Other methods less successful

2. There are some solutions to reduce or ____________________ these problems. They are ____________________ and take time to ____________________ and ____________________.

3. **(a)** What is meant by a "closed circuit" system?

____

____

____

(b) What are two major advantages to this system?

(i) ____

(ii) ____

Making the Best Use of the Land

p. 264

Read the instructions in question 36 on page 264 of the textbook. The map appears below. Answer questions (b), (c) and (d).

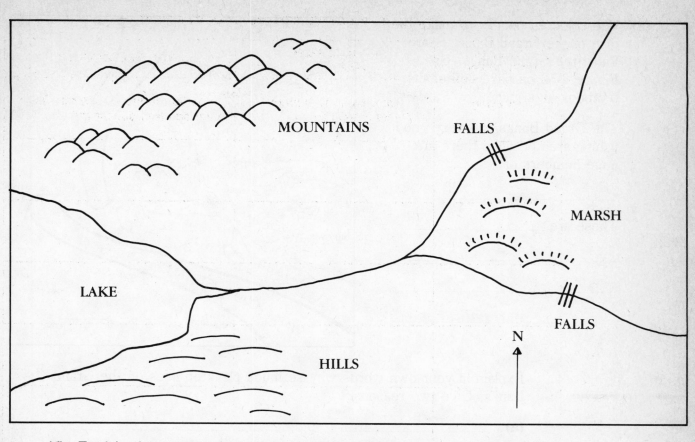

(d) Explain the reasons for your plan. Include reasons for rejecting the plans of some groups.

_____

_____

_____

_____

_____

_____

_____

_____

THE FISHING INDUSTRY

1. The three major exporters of fish, largest first, are _p. 265_

_____, _____, and

_____.

2. **(a)** Which is our most valuable fishing area? _____

(b) Which is our second most important fishing area? _____

(c) Where else do fish come from in Canada? _____

3. **(a)** Use coloured pencils to make the map of the Grand Banks clearer. Label the Grand Banks. Use Figure 8-52 on page 265 of the textbook as a guide.

   (b) The Grand Banks is a very good fishing area because there are huge numbers of

   _____.

   These are _____

   _____

   _____

   _____.

Map showing COLD LABRADOR CURRENT, Gulf of St. Lawrence, Newfoundland, New Brunswick, P.E.I., Nova Scotia, WARM GULF STREAM, Edge of the Continental Shelf, 0 300 km

p. 266

4. Explain in your own words why so much plankton lives on the Grand Banks. Give two reasons.

   (a) _____

   _____

   (b) _____

   _____

5. Why is the Grand Banks area the foggiest in the world? _____

   _____

6. Finish this diagram, using Figure 8-54 on page 266 of the textbook.

   Atlantic Ocean

FISHING OFF THE COAST OF THE ATLANTIC PROVINCES

p. 267

1. There are two major types of fishing in the Atlantic Ocean off Canada's east coast.

   (a) Inshore fishing is _____.

(b) Offshore fishing is _____.

2. Copy the table that describes inshore and offshore fishing which is found on page 267 of your textbook.

CHARACTERISTICS OF INSHORE FISHING	CHARACTERISTICS OF OFFSHORE FISHING

3. If you had the choice, would you prefer to fish inshore or offshore? Explain the reasons for your answer.

_____

_____

_____

_____

_____

FISHING METHODS AND FISH CAUGHT

p. 268

1. Fill in the blanks, following Figure 8-57 on page 268 of the textbook.

Three Important Fishing Methods

Purse Seining

A long net with _____ at the top and

_____ at the bottom is pulled into a

_____ around a _____ of fish. The

drawstring is pulled to _____ the

_____ of the net. The whole net is then

dragged toward the ship, and the fish are

_____ out with a large _____ net.

Purse seining catches fish that live _____

_____ of the

water, for example _____ and

_____.

(a)

Gill Netting

A net with floats on the _____ and weights

on the _____ is let out from the back of

the boat. The fish get _____ in the net and

are then hauled in. This method catches fish such

as _____ _____.

(b)

Otter Trawling (Dragnet Fishing)

A _____-_____ net held open by

wooden or metal "_____" is dragged along

the sea _____. The fish swim in and are

trapped in the _____ end. The net is hauled

on board where a special knot is untied to

_____ the fish on to the ship.

(c)

_____, _____, _____, and

_____ are all caught by otter trawling.

Each of these is a _____, which means

that it lives near the _____

_____ .

2. **(a)** Plot the figures shown in Figure 8-58 on page 268 of the textbook.
Label your graphs completely.

THE MOST VALUABLE TYPES OF FISH CAUGHT BY CANADIANS OFF THE
ATLANTIC COAST

Title: _____   Title: _____

(b) Which fish is the most valuable *per tonne*?
(Divide the tonnes into the value of the catch.)

Value of: cod per tonne   =
          lobster per tonne   =
          scallop per tonne   =
          queen crab per tonne =
          haddock per tonne   =

The most valuable fish per tonne is _____ .

SHELLFISH

p. 269

1. Describe how scallops live and how they are caught.

_____

_____

2. **(a)** Describe what a lobster pot is like. Sketch it if you can.

_____

_____

_____

_____

_____

(b) Why does a lobster get caught in the trap?

_____

_____

_____

p. 270

(c) Describe in your own words how the lobster fisher works.

_____

_____

_____

_____

_____

(d) Why is it important to throw some lobsters back?

_____

_____

THE PACIFIC COAST FISHERIES

p. 270

1. **(a)** Which is the most valuable west coast fish? _____

(b) Three other kinds of fish caught off the west coast are

_____, _____, and

_____.

2. Fill in the details from Figure 8-63 on page 270 of the textbook.

THE LIFE CYCLE OF THE PACIFIC SALMON

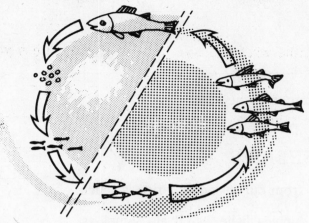

3. Why does the west coast provide such a suitable place for salmon to live? Give two reasons.

(a) _____

(b) _____

4. Salmon are caught by _____, _____ —,

or_____.

5. Describe trolling. _____

_____

_____

_____

6. Why has the number of salmon caught been declining? _____

_____

7. What two major efforts have been made to increase fish numbers?

p. 271

(a) _____

(b) _____

8. Look at Figure 8-65, on page 271 of the textbook. List the stages involved in producing and shipping a can of salmon until it gets onto a shelf in your home.

(a) salmon unloaded from ship

(b) _____

(c) _____

(d) _____

(e) _____

(f) _____

(g) _____

(h) salmon on home shelf

INLAND FISHERIES

p. 272

1. The catch from our inland fisheries is much _____ than that from our sea fisheries. It also employs _____ people.

2. Using an atlas map showing Canada's natural resources, list the places where most of our freshwater fish are caught, and name the kinds of fish caught.

PLACE	TYPE CAUGHT

PROTECTING OUR FISHERIES

pp. 272-273

1. How do we now exert control over the fish that live around our shores? List three ways.

   (a) _____

   (b) _____

   (c) _____

2. Why was it necessary to put more controls on fishing around our shores?

   _____

3. What else threatens our fish? Name two threats.

(a) _____

(b) _____

4. **(a)** Answer question 46 (a) on page 273 of the textbook.

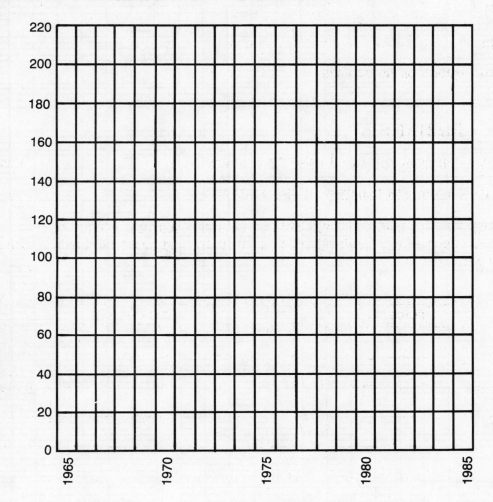

(b) What might have caused the variations in herring catch which are shown in your graph?

_____

_____

5. **(a)** What is a fish ladder? _____

_____

(b) What happens to fish if there are not fish ladders around dams? _____

_____

_____

VOCABULARY CROSSWORD

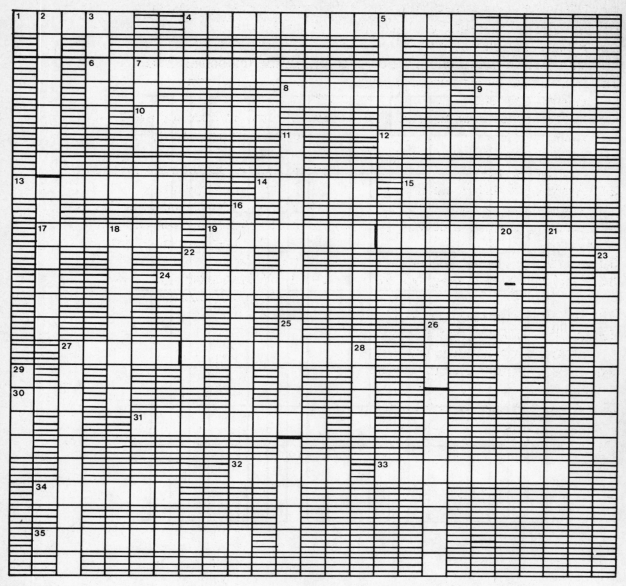

The answers are in the vocabulary on page 275 of the textbook and in Chapter 8.

Clues

ACROSS

1. A machine used to help pull fishing nets out of the water
4. Resources that cannot be regenerated
6. To dig
8. Partially processed iron ore
9. A purse _____ net traps fish near the surface.

DOWN

2. Working the waters close to shore (two words)
3. _____ cutting is when all the trees in an area are cut down.
5. The ability to reach a place
7. A cylindrical sample of rock
11. To use up a resource
16. Furniture is _____ from wood.

10. Mineral _____ have to be obtained before mining starts.
12. When only certain trees are cut, it is called _____ cutting.
13. Fishing in deep water
14. The vertical tunnel in a mine
15. Money paid by a mining company to a government
17. Large cavities in an underground mine
19. Naturally formed objects that we use (two words)
24. Assigning a certain amount of production to a mine
27. Catching fish with a dragnet (two words)
30. A valuable mineral deposit
31. Machines used to drag logs from the woods
32. Another word meaning "open pit"
33. A fishing method that involves dragging hooks behind the boat
34. _____ fish live near the bottom of the sea.
35. Resources that can regenerate themselves

18. Living fish food
20. To replenish stocks that are getting low (one word, hyphenated)
21. To make use of
22. Horizontal tunnels in an underground mine
23. A counting
25. The lowest price for which a commodity may be sold (two words)
26. A country that imports more than it exports (two words)
27. The non-valuable material that is over valuable mineral deposits
28. _____ nets catch many fish near the surface.
29. A 370 km fishing _____ is controlled by Canada.

9

CANADA'S INDUSTRIES

PERSONAL PROGRESS CHART

Put a check mark in the first square for each section when your teacher assigns it. When you have completed the section, put a check mark in the second square.

Page	Topic	Assigned by teacher	Completed by you
235	Canadian Industry	☐	☐
235	Types of Industry	☐	☐
237	Factors That Affect the Location of Industries	☐	☐
239	The Importance of the Great Lakes – St. Lawrence Seaway	☐	☐
242	The Location of the Aluminum Industry	☐	☐
243	Steel Production in Canada	☐	☐
246	Treating and Using Wastes	☐	☐
246	Employee Relations	☐	☐
246	The Automobile Industry	☐	☐
250	Small Business Operations	☐	☐
250	Restaurants — A Tertiary Industry	☐	☐
251	McDonald's Restaurants	☐	☐
253	Vocabulary Crossword	☐	☐

CANADIAN INDUSTRY

1. Industry occurs wherever a _____ or

   _____ is provided.

p. 277

2. The owner of an industry attempts to make a _____.

3. The text says that the profit motive is essential to Canada's whole

   economy. Explain why the profit motive is so important. _____

   _____

   _____

TYPES OF INDUSTRY

1. Complete the following chart with manufactured items you can find in your
   classroom.

p. 278

MANUFACTURED ITEM	NAME OF MANUFACTURER	MATERIALS USED IN PRODUCING ITEM	TYPES OF TRANSPORTATION THAT COULD HAVE BROUGHT THE ITEM FROM MANUFACTURER TO YOUR SCHOOL
Pen	Bic	Plastic, steel, ink	Truck

2. **(a)** There are three major categories of industry in Canada. Fit them into the following diagram. Fill in the outside ring only.

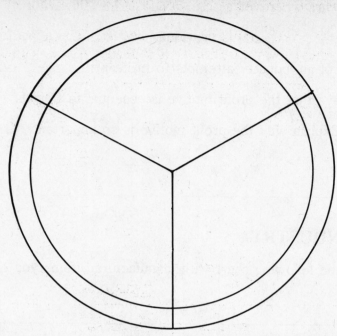

(b) Fit these occupations into the correct industrial category in the diagram above: miner, postal worker, sales clerk, tailor, farm worker, steelworker, hunter, dress designer, politician.

3. Use Figure 9-3 and Figure 9-4 on pages 278 and 279 to answer these questions.

(a) Rank the ten most important manufacturing centres, largest first.

(i) _____ **(v)** _____ **(viii)** _____

(ii) _____ **(vi)** _____ **(ix)** _____

(iii) _____ **(vii)** _____ **(x)** _____

(iv) _____

(b) In which parts of which provinces is most Canadian manufacturing

located? _____

_____

_____

4. **(a)** When you leave school, in what category of industry would you likely

get a job? _____

(b) Explain the reasons for your answer. _____

_____

_____

FACTORS THAT AFFECT THE LOCATION OF INDUSTRIES

Read the section in the textbook from pages 280 to 281.

1. Each section in the diagram represents one location factor. Name each factor and write a short description of it in the section provided.

p. 281

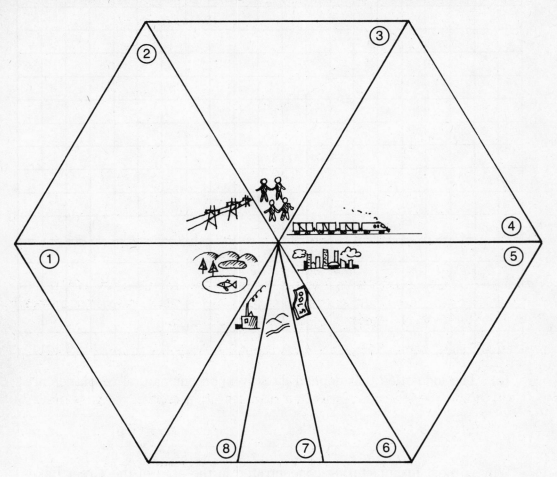

2. In your own words, explain what is meant by "value added"; use your own example.

_____

_____

3. Answer question 7 on page 282 in the textbook.

   (a) The order of value added in manufacturing industries is

   (i) _____   (vi) _____

   (ii) _____   (vii) _____

   (iii) _____   (viii) _____

   (iv) _____   (ix) _____

   (v) _____   (x) _____

(b) Plot a bar graph to show the ranking of value added. Make up your own scale.

VALUE ADDED BY THE TEN LARGEST MANUFACTURING INDUSTRIES

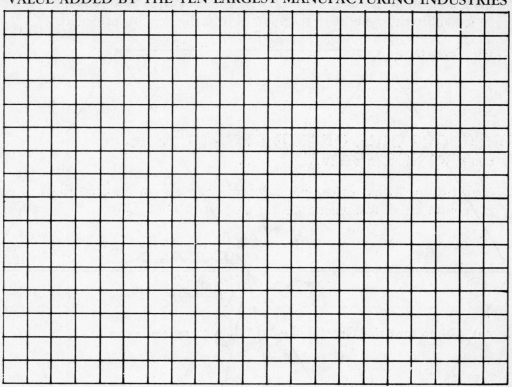

(c) The industries that depend directly upon our natural resources are _____

_____

_____ .

4. Why is most manufacturing concentrated in the area of the Great Lakes–St. Lawrence Seaway? An atlas will help you. Break your answer into the following sections:

(a) Closeness to raw materials _____

_____

_____

_____

(b) Power _____

_____

(c) Labour _____

_____

(d) Transportation _____

_____

_____

(e) Market _____

_____

THE IMPORTANCE OF THE GREAT LAKES–
ST. LAWRENCE SEAWAY

1. How has the Great Lakes–St. Lawrence Seaway encouraged the concentration of manufacturing in that part of the country?

p. 282

_____

_____

_____

2. **(a)** When was the Great Lakes–St. Lawrence Seaway opened?

_____

(b) How much did it cost? _____

(c) Who paid for it? _____

3. **(a)** What is a canal? _____

(b) Canals by-pass rapids and falls. What does "by-pass" mean? _____

_____

What are rapids? _____

4. **(a)** What is dredging? _____

(b) Why is dredging necessary? _____

_____

5. What is the minimum depth of all parts of the Seaway? _____ m

6. Finish this diagram, using Figure 9-6 on page 282 in your textbook as a guide.

OBSTACLES TO BE OVERCOME IN THE GREAT LAKES AND ST. LAWRENCE RIVER

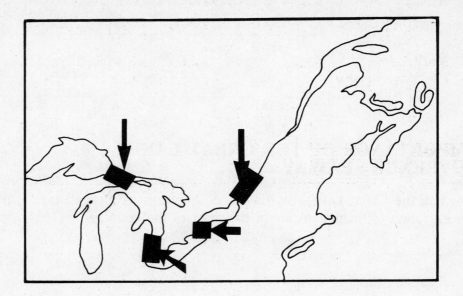

p. 283

7. (a) Copy below the sequence of diagrams in Figure 9-8 on page 283 in the textbook.

HOW A LOCK IS USED

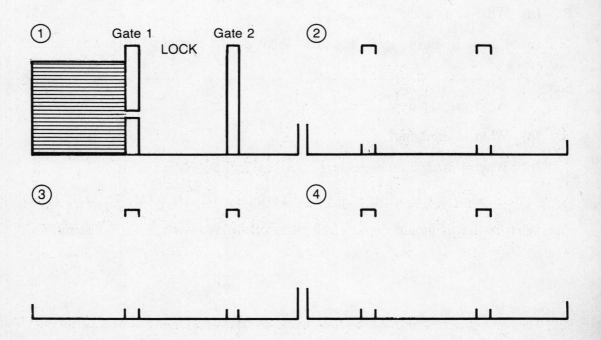

(b) Use four diagrams to show how you would use a lock to get a ship upstream. The first one is drawn for you. (You can only change the height of the water in the lock between Gate 1 and Gate 2.)

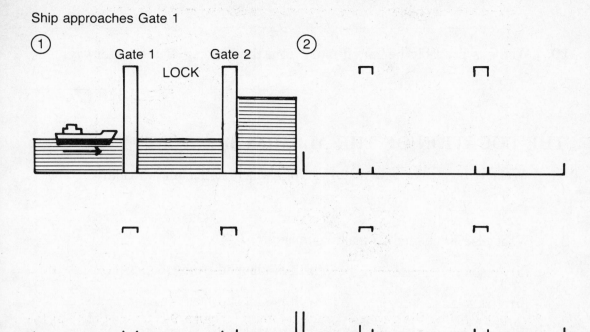

Ship approaches Gate 1

8. Finish this diagram using Figure 9-9 on page 284 of the textbook as a guide.

A PROFILE OF THE GREAT LAKES-ST. LAWRENCE WATERWAY

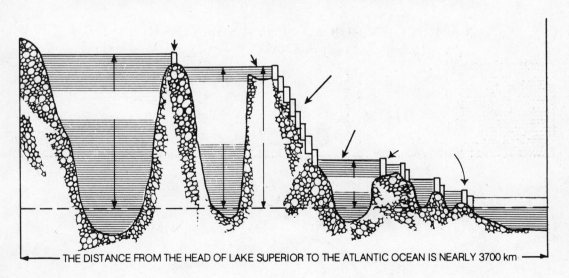

THE DISTANCE FROM THE HEAD OF LAKE SUPERIOR TO THE ATLANTIC OCEAN IS NEARLY 3700 km

9. How is some of the cost of building the waterway being recovered? Explain each way briefly. *p. 284*

(a) _____

(b) _____

_____

10. Who has probably benefited most from the building of the waterway? _____

_____

THE LOCATION OF THE ALUMINUM INDUSTRY

p. 284

1. What is the major raw material from which aluminum is made?

_____

2. What else is needed to make aluminum?

(a) _____ which is shipped from _____

(b) _____ which is shipped from _____

3. Why are large quantities of electricity required?

_____

_____

p. 285

4. Answer question 13 (a) at the top of page 285 in the textbook. Use the map below.

LOCATION OF MAJOR ALUMINUM SMELTERS IN EASTERN CANADA

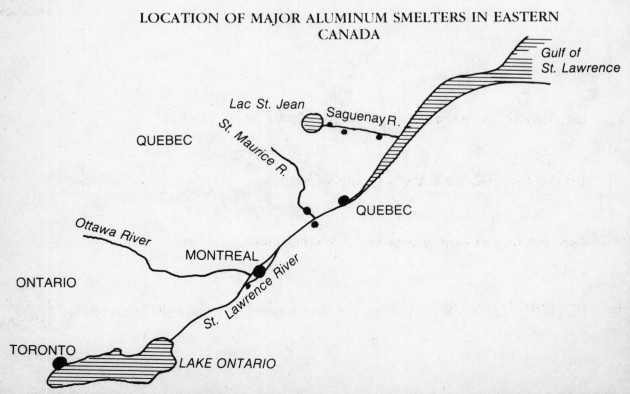

5. Answer question 13 (b) on page 285 of the textbook. Use this table for your answer. Put a check mark in the column where each location has an advantage.

ALUMINUM SMELTER	CLOSE TO RAW MATERIALS	POWER	LABOUR	TRANSPORTATION	MARKET
Jonquière					
La Baie					
Alma					
Shawinigan					
Beauharnois					
Bécancour					

6. Could an aluminum smelter be located near where you live? _____

Explain your answer. _____

_____

_____

_____

STEEL PRODUCTION IN CANADA

1. What is the major difference between iron and steel? *p. 285*

_____

_____

_____

2. (a) Why is the iron and steel industry called a heavy industry?

_____

(b) Give two other examples of heavy industry: _____ and

_____

3. Give two of your own examples of a light industry: _____

and _____

4. (a) What is smelting? _____ *p. 288*

_____

(b) What is refining? _____

_____

p. 288

5. Fill in the labels. To make one tonne of liquid iron takes:

ONE TONNE
OF LIQUID IRON

6. Fill in the following table. Figure 9-12 on page 288 in the textbook and your atlas will help.

RAW MATERIAL		DISTANCE TRAVELLED TO HAMILTON (km)	METHOD(S) OF TRANSPORTATION
IRON ORE	from Labrador		
	from Northern Ontario		
LIMESTONE from Ingersoll, Ontario			
COAL from West Virginia, U.S.A.			

p. 289

7. Answer question 16 on page 289 in the textbook.

_____

_____

_____

_____

8. **(a)** What is meant by stockpiled? _____

_____

(b) Why is it necessary to stockpile iron ore from Labrador and coal from

West Virginia each summer? _____

_____

9. Why is more Canadian coal not used? _____

_____

10. Finish the following sentences. Your account will be a description of how steel is made.

pp. 286-287

The three major ingredients for steelmaking are _____,

_____, and _____. Iron ore pellets are

usually made close to the iron ore mines. Each is a heavy grey ball about

_____ cm across (see Figure 8-15 on page 246). Coal is

first made into coke by _____.

The three ingredients are loaded into the top of the tall _____

furnace, using a _____ car. Inside the furnace the ore is

changed to liquid _____, which settles to the bottom. The

limestone joins with _____ to form _____,

which floats on the top of the iron. When there is enough iron it is allowed

to flow out into a huge _____.

Liquid iron is mixed with _____ in a _____

_____ furnace, where it becomes steel in less than an

_____. _____ is blown onto the surface

of the liquid steel in the furnace to burn out _____. The

steel is then poured into a _____ and from the ladle into

_____ moulds.

After about 25 minutes the moulds are stripped off, leaving hot

_____, which are then kept in a hot _____

pit. In the soaking pit the temperature of the ingot is kept suitable for rolling.

The ingot is then transported to the _____ mills, where it is

rolled backward and forward at great speeds until it is of the correct thickness.

It is then rolled up, as in the last photograph of the steelmaking process shown

on page 287, and tied securely for transportation.

TREATING AND USING WASTES

p. 290

1. Read the section on page 290 in the textbook.
    List seven ways in which the steel companies in Hamilton reduce pollution.

    (a) _____

    (b) _____

    (c) _____

    (d) _____

    (e) _____

    (f) _____

    (g) _____

EMPLOYEE RELATIONS

p. 291

1. Read the section "Employee Relations" on page 291 in your textbook.
    In what ways would the measures outlined be beneficial to:

    (a) the company and its shareholders _____

    _____

    _____

    (b) the employees _____

    _____

    _____

    (c) its suppliers and customers _____

    _____

    _____

    (d) the community in general _____

    _____

    _____

THE AUTOMOBILE INDUSTRY

p. 291

1. **(a)** How many people are directly employed in making cars, trucks, and
        their parts?

        _____

(b) List ten other types of work that depend on the automobile industry.

(i) _____   **(v)** _____   **(viii)** _____

(ii) _____   **(vi)** _____   **(ix)** _____

(iii) _____   **(vii)** _____   **(x)** _____

(iv) _____

2. Answer question 22 (a) on pages 291 and 292 of the textbook.

The Percentage of Our
Total Expenses Used
for Transportation

How Our Transportation
Costs Are Divided Up

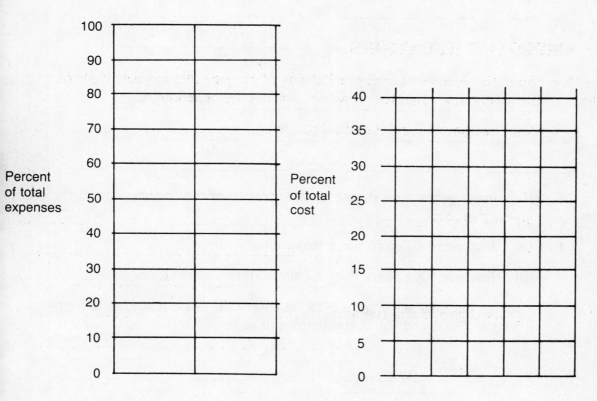

3. Answer question 22 (b) on page 292 of the textbook.

_____

_____

_____

4. Look at Figure 9-17 on page 292 of the textbook. List the materials used to make a car, under these headings.

METALS	NATURAL PRODUCTS	SYNTHETIC PRODUCTS
Chromium	Rubber	Plastic

5. How many years does it take to get a car from the original idea to the final production stage? _____

6. **(a)** How many different parts make up one car? _____

   (b) How many suppliers does General Motors depend on? _____

7. Look at the map and Figure 9-19 on page 293 of the textbook and answer question 23 (a) and (b) at the bottom of page 293 of the textbook.

   (a) _____

   _____

   (b) _____

   _____

   _____

   _____

8. **(a)** What is an assembly line? _____

   _____

(b) Why is it necessary to have a steady flow of parts for an assembly line?

_____

_____

9. Answer question 25 (a) and (b) at the bottom of page 294 of your textbook. _p. 294_

(a) _____

_____

(b) _____

_____

10. Design your own car.

(a) In this space, draw the shape of the car of your dreams.

(b) List the special features your car would have (types of seats, upholstery, steering wheel, air conditioning, radio, stereo, and so on).

_____

_____

_____

_____

_____

_____

_____

_____

_____

_____

SMALL BUSINESS OPERATIONS

p. 295

1. Why are small businesses also called cottage industries? _____

_____

_____

2. Read the story of the stained glass business. List five different types of activities that you think would be suitable for a cottage industry.

(a) _____   (d) _____

(b) _____   (e) _____

(c) _____

p. 296

3. Answer question 29 from page 296 of the textbook.

_____

_____

_____

_____

_____

_____

_____

_____

_____

RESTAURANTS — A TERTIARY INDUSTRY

pp. 296-297

1. Read the section about food services on pages 296 to 297 of the textbook.

Give two reasons why more and more meals are being eaten away from home.

(a) _____

(b) _____

2. (a) What is your favourite fast-food meal?

_____

(b) Where do you get it?

_____

McDONALD'S RESTAURANTS

1. What is a "multi-national" organization? p. 298

_____

2. Why do many companies and businesses, like McDonald's, sell shares?

_____

_____

3. **(a)** What is a franchise system? _____

_____

(b) How much does it cost to get a McDonald's franchise? $ _____

4. Look at the six photographs on pages 298 and 299 in the textbook. Identify _pp. 298-299_
where each one comes from. Choose from England, Bahamas, Hong Kong,
Austria, Japan, and Australia. Give reasons for each answer.

COUNTRY	PHOTOGRAPH (PAGE AND POSITION)	REASONS
England		
Bahamas		
Hong Kong		
Austria		
Japan		
Australia		

5. Answer question 34 at the top of page 300 in the textbook.

(34) **(a)** The amount of money sent each year to the U.S. headquarters

for the use of an average McDonald's building is

$ _____.

(b) The amount of money spent on advertising each year is

$ _____ per McDonald's store.

(c) The average franchise owner earns $ _____ per
year.

Copyright © 1987 John Wiley & Sons Canada Limited   9/Canada's Industries **251**

6. How does a McDonald's Restaurant help the community around it? _____

_____

_____

_____

_____

7. Imagine that you had enough money to start your own fast-food outlet. What foods would you offer and what other special attractions would you design into your restaurant?

_____

_____

_____

_____

_____

_____

_____

_____

_____

_____

_____

VOCABULARY CROSSWORD

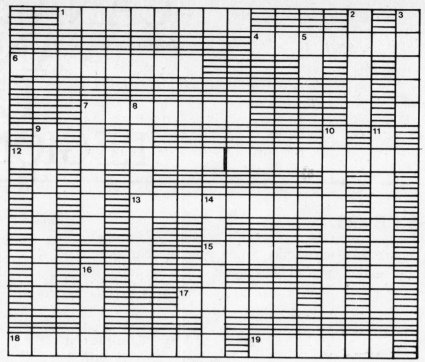

The answers are in the vocabulary on page 301 of the textbook and in Chapter 9.

Clues

ACROSS

1. The first stage in processing a mineral
4. Aluminum ore
6. Making iron into steel is called _____.
7. Agriculture, fishing, and mining are examples of _____ industry.
12. Manufacturing is also called _____ _____. (two words)
13. A huge reserve of material
15. A charge made for using a canal, bridge, or road
17. A man-made river
18. You need a _____ to operate a McDonald's Restaurant.
19. The profit _____ encourages people to work.

DOWN

2. An industry that uses small machinery
3. Steelmaking is a _____ industry.
5. Ships moving toward the source of a river are _____ bound.
7. The money that remains after all costs are paid
8. Work that produces a valuable product or service
9. Services are _____ industry.
10. The _____ line is an efficient method of manufacturing.
11. Deepening water channels by digging the mud out
14. Small-scale industry
16. Materials moving toward the mouth of a river are called _____ bound.

10 CANADA AND ITS REGIONS

PERSONAL PROGRESS CHART

Put a check mark in the first square for each section when your teacher assigns it. When you have completed the section, put a check mark in the second square.

Page	Topic	Assigned by teacher	Completed by you
254	Introduction	☐	☐
255	Canada's Political Growth	☐	☐
256	Regional Studies of Canada	☐	☐
261	Economic Differences	☐	☐
263	French-English Differences	☐	☐
264	Canada's Pattern of Physical Features	☐	☐
266	The Importance of Communications to Canada and Its People	☐	☐
267	Canada Challenge Crossword	☐	☐

INTRODUCTION

p. 303

Match each region in the left column with the correct description in the right column. Use lines to join the regions and the correct description(s).

REGION	DESCRIPTION
Atlantic Provinces	Highest population
Quebec	Southern part is grassland
	Few inhabitants
Ontario	Very rugged, forested landscape
	Mainly mountains
Prairies	Coast lies along Atlantic Ocean
British Columbia	Most industrialized
	Generally cold climate
Yukon and Northwest Territories	French is predominant language
	Largely flat land
	Mostly forested with rugged, rocky landscape

CANADA'S POLITICAL GROWTH

1. Canada has become a _____ - _____   *p. 304*

   Dominion in just over _____ years. From the original four provinces

   of _____ , _____ ,

   _____ , and _____ , Canada has

   expanded across North America.

2. In 1867 the _____ (_____) Act was introduced   *p. 305*

   to give Canada three basic levels of government. The largest was the

   _____ (_____) _____ , which

   was to handle _____

   and _____ .

      This BNA Act is considered to be the _____ . It

   recognized both _____ and _____ as official

   _____ in Canada. In 1982 Canada gained the right to

   change its constitution.

REGIONAL STUDIES OF CANADA

In Chapter 2 you completed maps of Canada's regions with their cities, rivers, lakes, and so on. Here are maps of Canada's five political regions. On each one, mark the following and include a key:

1. the provinces and territories

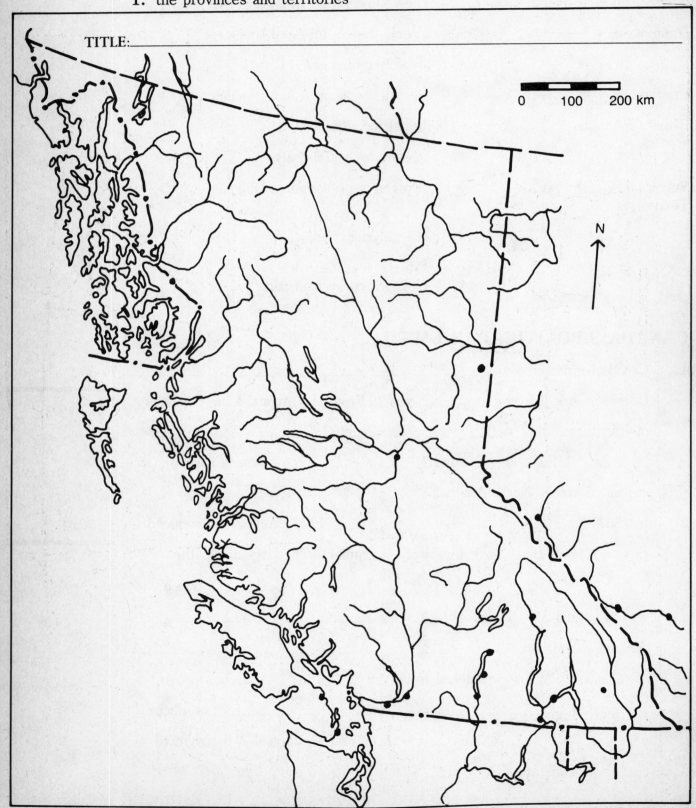

TITLE:

0 100 200 km

N

2. major bodies of water and rivers
3. major highways and railways
4. major ports
5. major mining centres
6. important areas for agriculture (Label the individual types of agriculture of the region.)
7. important centres of industry (Be sure to label the types of industry in each city.)

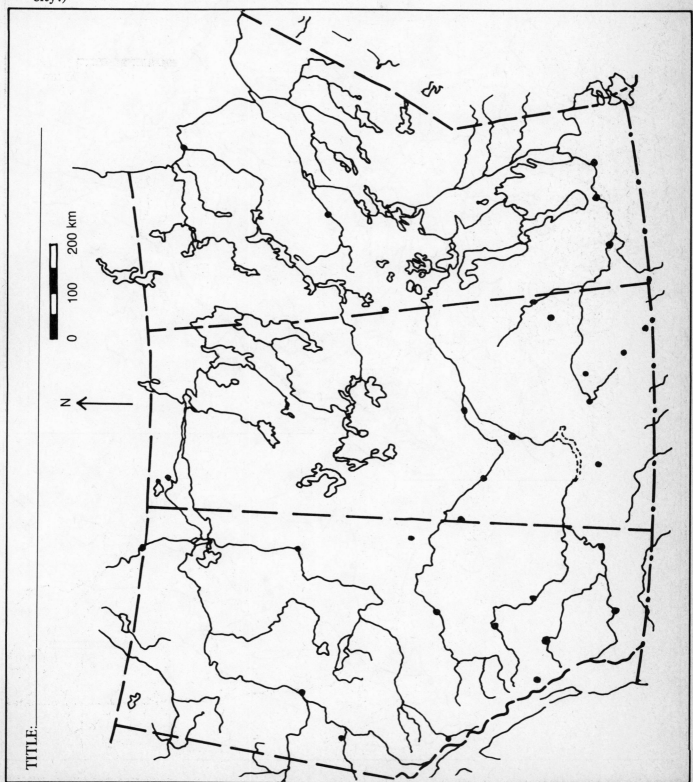

TITLE:

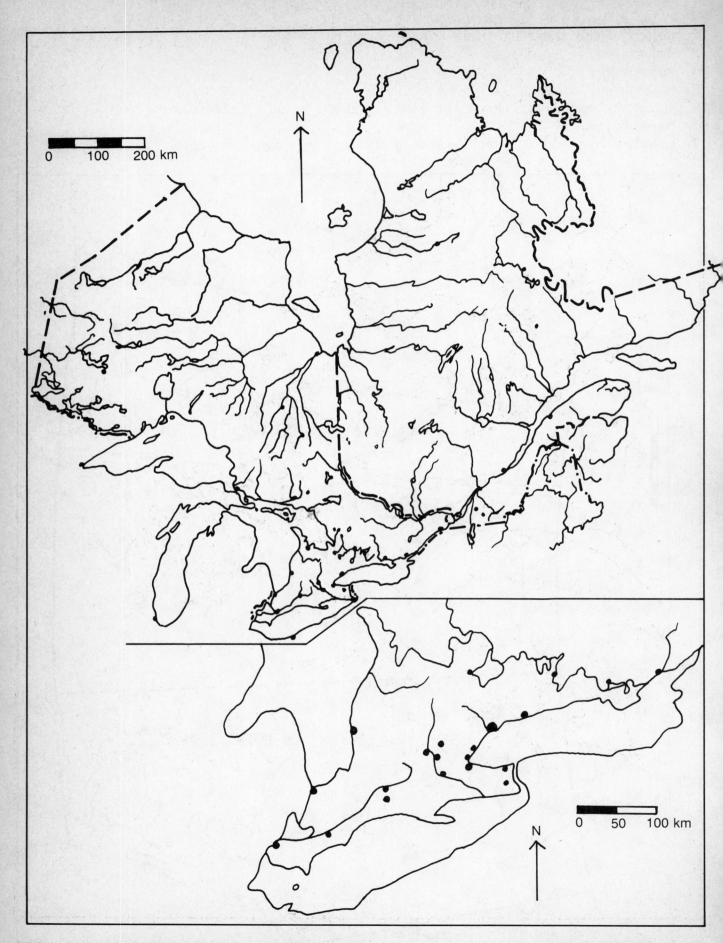

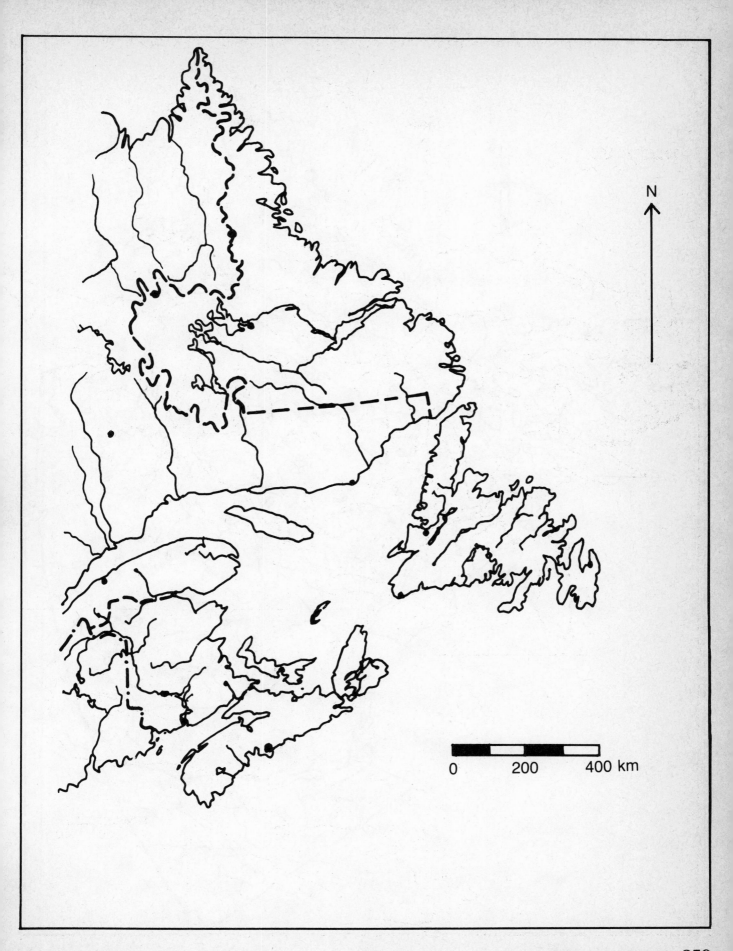

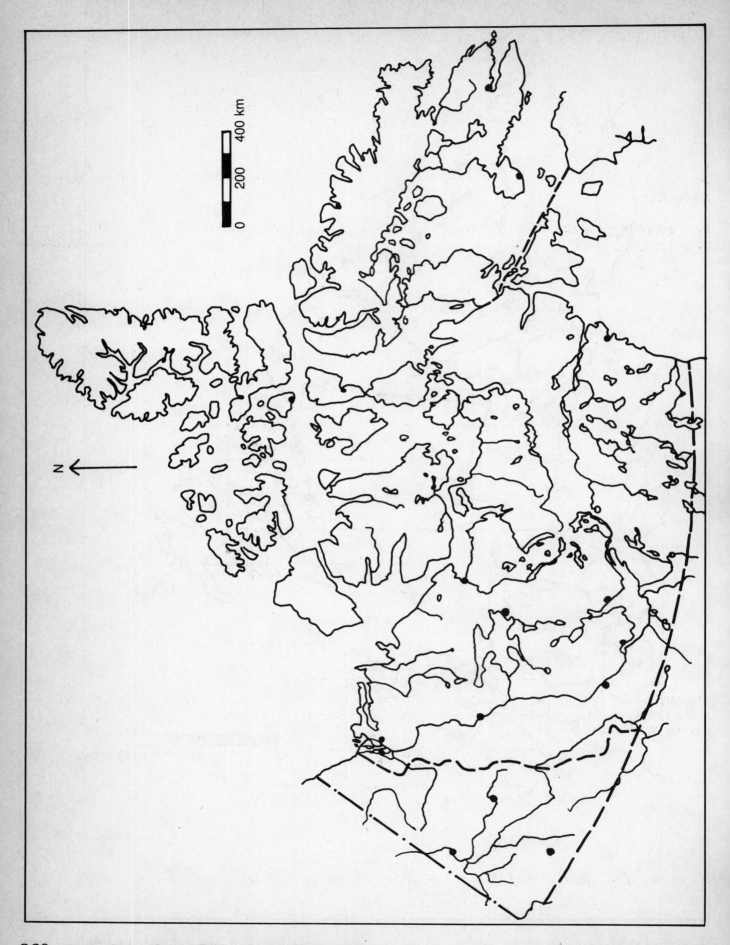

ECONOMIC DIFFERENCES

Region of Canada	Average Income per Person (1985)	Unemployment (1985) (as a percentage of the work force)
Atlantic Provinces	15 000	14.0
Quebec	14 500	8.6
Ontario	17 000	8.2
Prairies	11 500	12.0
British Columbia	15 600	16.0

1. Answer questions 12 and 13 from page 307 in the textbook using the statistics given here.

p. 307

    (12) **(a)**

Title:_____

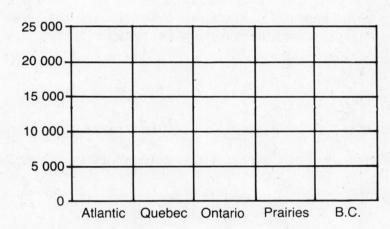

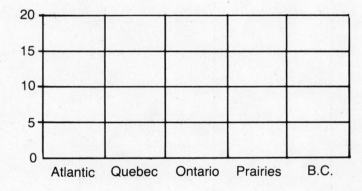

    (b) The region of Canada that appears to have the healthiest economy

    is _____ .

The evidence for this is _____

_____

_____

_____ .

(13) Which other statistics besides unemployment and income can you think of

that would show economic differences within Canada? _____

_____

_____

_____

2. Read the section at the bottom of page 307 in the textbook. Imagine that
you are the logger. Use the space below to write the letter to the
environmentalist in Moncton, New Brunswick.

_____
Date

Dear Friend:

    This letter is to inform you of some of the concerns that I have about my life,

job, and way of life. For example, I am interested in _____

_____

_____

_____

_____

_____

_____

_____

_____

_____

_____

            Yours sincerely,

_____
(your name)

3. Fill in the blanks.

p. 308

The _____ government has also set up a program

of _____ to the provinces. These payments take

_____ from the _____ provinces

and give it to the _____ provinces.

FRENCH-ENGLISH DIFFERENCES

1. **(a)** Explain each of the following terms in your own words.

pp. 308-309

Mother tongue _____

_____

Separatism _____

_____

_____

Québécois _____

_____

(b) Write a few sentences below, using these three terms to explain some basic facts about Quebec and Canada.

_____

_____

_____

_____

_____

_____

_____

_____

_____

_____

p. 309

2. Using the following chart, match each of the complaints from Quebec with efforts to hold Canada together.

QUEBEC'S COMPLAINTS	EFFORTS TO HOLD CANADA TOGETHER

CANADA'S PATTERN OF PHYSICAL FEATURES

p. 310

1. Using the map on page 310 of the textbook, complete the map of North America below, showing the major physical regions. Colour each region *lightly*, as you will be using the map for other purposes later.

2. The orientation of most of the regions of North America is generally _____
_____ .

3. Answer question 17 (b), (c), and (d) from page 310 in the textbook.

(17) **(b)** Based on physical features, North American countries would be
oriented from _____ to _____ .

(c) Answer this question using the map of North America.

(d) The advantages of my arrangement would be _____
_____
_____ .

The disadvantages might be _____
_____

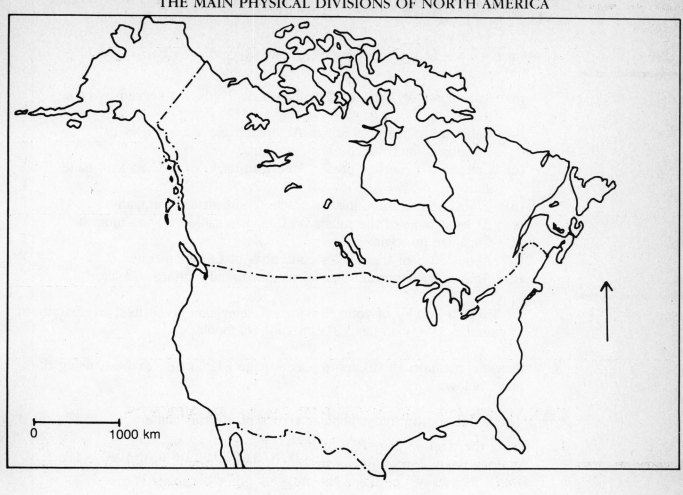

_____

_____ .

4.   Answer question 18 from page 310 in the textbook.

_____

_____

_____

_____

_____

_____

_____

THE IMPORTANCE OF COMMUNICATIONS TO CANADA AND ITS PEOPLE

p. 311

1. Answer each of the following questions by circling either T (True) or F (False).

   (a) Approximately 80% of Canadian households are served by cable television.   T   F

   (b) Cable television also brings American television shows to Canadians far from the U.S. border.   T   F

   (c) Canadians generally prefer American-made over Canadian-made shows.   T   F

   (d) CRTC stands for Canadian Radio Transmitting Company.   T   F

   (e) At least 50% of the music on Canadian radio stations must be Canadian in origin.   T   F

   (f) About 80% of the CBC's content is of Canadian origin.   T   F

p. 312

   (g) *Anik* is an important Canadian telecommunications satellite.   T   F

2. Complete a survey of your classmates' television favourites, as described in question 19 (a) on page 312 in your textbook.

3. Answer question 19 (b) and (c) from page 312 in the textbook using the chart below.

   These are the ten most popular shows of my classmates:

   SHOWS   COUNTRY OF ORIGIN (CANADA, U.S.A., OR ELSEWHERE)

   (a) _____   _____

   (b) _____   _____

   (c) _____   _____

   (d) _____   _____

   (e) _____   _____

   (f) _____   _____

   (g) _____   _____

   (h) _____   _____

   (i) _____   _____

   (j) _____   _____

4. Answer question 19 (d) on page 312 in the textbook.

   This survey shows that the United States influences Canadians by _____

   _____

5. Write a short paragraph to explain how Canadians communicate with each other.

_____

_____

_____

_____

_____

_____

CANADA CHALLENGE CROSSWORD

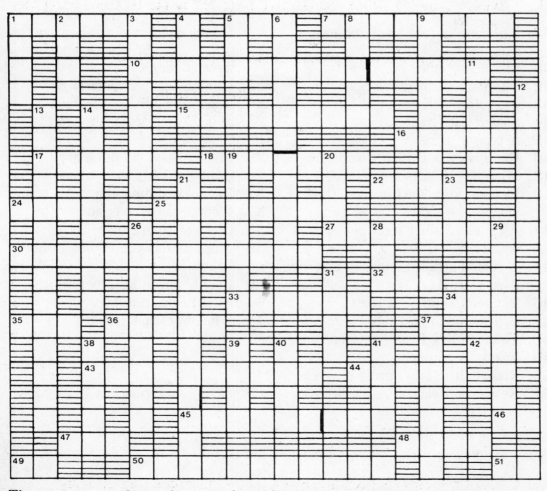

The answers to these clues are found in all parts of the book. For some you might need your atlas.

Clues

ACROSS

1. Population density in the Arctic is very _____ .
5. Our largest trading partner
7. Cars are made on one of these lines.
10. A road with shops, gas stations, restaurants, and so on (two words)
15. 23.5°S is the Tropic of _____ .
16. The passenger pigeon is an _____ .
17. Horizontal tunnels in a mine
18. Capital of Ontario
22. Where pulp is made and ore is processed
24. Villages grow into _____ .
25. Canadian city with second largest population
27. Lines measuring west and east from 0°
30. Secondary industry
32. The number of provinces
33. Capital of Canada
34. Shallowest Great Lake
35. A type of mine
36. Deep inlet in British Columbia
42. Mini _____ means lowest.
43. Floating logs down a river (two words)
44. A chunk of solid steel before it is rolled
45. A rule controlling building in a city (two words)
46. Between south and west
47. British North America
48. Thunder Bay is an important one.
49. Yukon Territory
50. Rock that usually forms in layers
51. New Brunswick

DOWN

1. Podzol is one kind.
2. Short form for one program designed to help farmers
3. To dig a large hole
4. Built to create a reservoir
5. Simple word meaning ''exploit''
6. Our northern water body (two words)
8. Energy from the sun
9. Poor farmland
11. 0° Meridian
12. Many industries _____ the air and water.
13. Dangerous emissions from a nuclear plant are called _____ .
14. A unit of land in Quebec
19. Province with the most people
20. One way of getting money back for the St. Lawrence Seaway
21. _____ freight is a cheaper way of moving cargo.
23. Land division in Ontario
26. Important port on the Pacific
28. Short form for Northwest Territories
29. Maple, oak, and birch are examples of _____ trees.
31. Hills near Edmonton
37. Wearing away the land
38. City environment
39. Much of this ore comes from Labrador.
40. Coal is put in here before it is used to make iron.
41. Winter precipitation